THE
MODERN
CHEESEBOARD

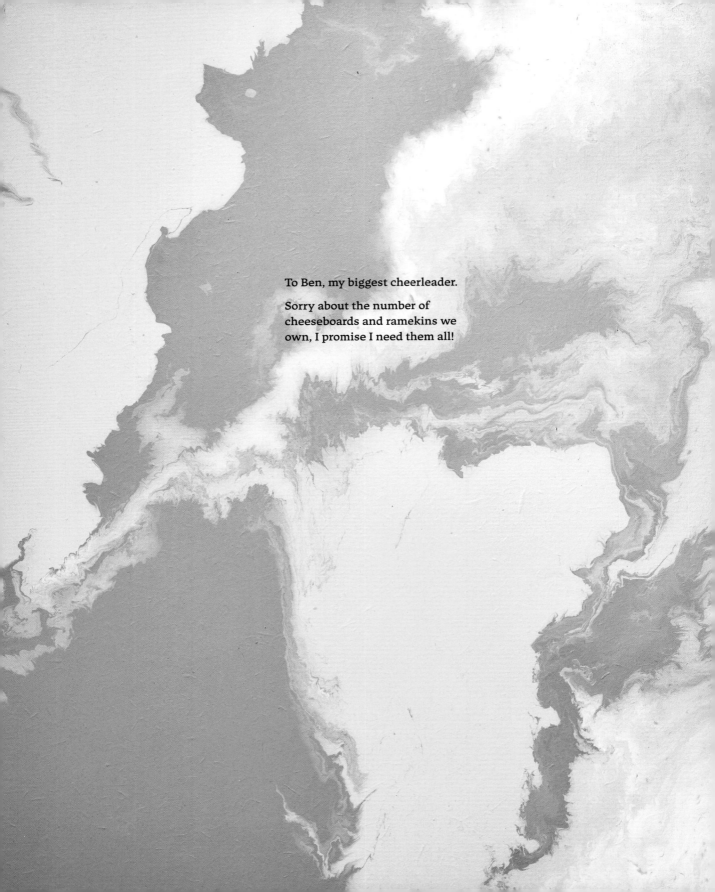

To Ben, my biggest cheerleader.

Sorry about the number of
cheeseboards and ramekins we
own, I promise I need them all!

Morgan
McGlynn

THE
MODERN
CHEESEBOARD

Pair your way to the perfect
grazing platter

WHITE LION
PUBLISHING

06   Introduction

38   EVERYDAY

78   THROUGHOUT
        THE YEAR

110   AROUND
        THE WORLD

134   SHOWSTOPPER

158   RECIPES FOR
        THE BOARDS

166   The Best Cheese Shops from
        Around the World

172   Index

176   Acknowledgements

INTRODUCTION

My World of Cheese

My life has been consumed by cheese for over 14 years, in the best possible way, since I opened my little cheese shop in Muswell Hill, north London.

I spend my days talking about cheese and teaching people which cheeses work together, what pairs well with what and how easy and simple (yet incredibly satisfying) it is to create the perfect cheeseboard to wow loved ones and guests.

Before owning my shop, I studied graphic design and have always been a very visual person; aesthetics are really important to me. Good cheese speaks for itself, but a good cheeseboard makes the experience of eating cheese – which, let's face it, we all love already – that little bit more special.

Gone are the days when a selection of cheese was laid haphazardly on a presentation board. This book is here to ensure your next party is a success – and the key? Cheese grazing boards!

As any seasoned host will tell you, a well-put-together cheeseboard is a foolproof crowd-pleaser. A humble wooden board full of good cheese and fresh produce can so easily become the most impressive, extravagant part of a meal, party or gathering.

I started making cheeseboards when I was 20 years old and I would take them to friends and family when visiting: the boards were a creative outlet for me and started as a hobby. As the years went on, however, and I opened my cheese shop, customers would ask me if I could put together boards for them and this became an extension of my business.

A few years back I was very poorly and unable to work in the shop for several months. I found myself at home with nothing to do, so I put together cheeseboards. I missed being in my shop and this was a creative outlet for me to keep busy doing something I really loved.

Over the years I have created hundreds of custom sharing cheeseboards, from a cosy two-person board to full grazing tables for 200-plus people. They have ranged massively depending on the occasion, whether it be seasonal, to focusing on a certain colour scheme, place, theme or event. Whatever the board, guests are always wowed by the concept of sharing a gorgeous eye-catching plate of the best produce out there, tempting guests to explore an array of culinary wonders.

In the last few years, the popularity of the cheeseboard has gone through the roof, but these gorgeous boards all over Instagram can seem unrealistic or unapproachable, and knowing what goes where and how all the elements work together can seem tricky. I think there is an art to the board looking beautiful, while also getting that cheese pairing right. This book will show you that it's actually much more achievable than you think. The magic that can happen with the perfect pairings is only a few steps away.

There are few things that bring as much joy on a table as a beautifully designed cheeseboard and doing it well is an art form. This book will guide you step by step through the process, to create cheeseboards full of incredible sweet and savoury produce and seasonal cheeses, with drinks pairings suggestions throughout. The cherry on top? All these things come together to result in an Insta-worthy, showstopping cheeseboard for your next dinner party, wine nights with friends, or an evening of self-indulgence.

Getting Started

The board

The board itself is the foundation of any perfect cheeseboard. No matter the material; that cheeseboard is full of stories of parties gone by. I love to use natural materials such as wood, marble and slate: they work so well for food. Of course, porcelain plates, glass and metal also work. The board is a base for your ingredients to be displayed on, so go with whatever you have to hand.

Classic wooden cheeseboard

Most cheese lovers' kitchen cupboards contain a wooden cheeseboard. Wooden boards are great, as they are easy to clean, look great and are resistant to stains.

Boards come in every shape and size imaginable, but my go-to board tends to be the classic round 55 cm (22 inch) middle-of-the-table showstopper. This is the board to use for parties: fill it right up to the brim for a generous display and let the sharing begin. If you've got a lazy Susan version, even better! For parties, you could also opt for a grazing table set-up (page 154).

Long tapas board

Another favourite of mine. This is great to place along the centre of the table for a sit-down dinner, laying out the delicious delights all the way along the table so they're within everyone's grasp.

Old wooden chopping board

No glitz and glamour here, just an old reliable and hard-wearing chopping board. It might be scratched and worn, but it's full of charm. I love hardy old boards so much, and they are well suited for a small selection of cheeses.

To ensure your wooden board lasts a lifetime, wash it with water, then dip half a lemon into coarse salt and rub this over the board, then rinse and dry. When dry, rub oil into the board using kitchen paper: walnut, olive, almond or coconut oil work best. This keeps the board in good condition.

The board is a base for your ingredients... so go with whatever you have to hand

Slate board

Slate boards are some of the most naturally durable and resilient boards out there and they're becoming more and more widely available: I have bought high-end boards from home interior shops and found more reasonably priced ones in kitchenware shops. Slate is a fantastic material as it is non-porous, which means it less prone to stain, mark or discolour. And the added bonus it that it's super easy to clean.

Cheesemonger Tip

If you would like to get creative with your slate board, use chalk to draw and write labels or tasting suggestions on the board for a novel way to present the cheeses. This is great for a party.

Marble board

Marble boards are so chic, beautiful and stylish, and are one of my go-to bases for a cheeseboard. The natural surface is perfect for serving on, and it's cool, so is ideal for serving food outside on warmer days. However, marble can mark easily so I often place greaseproof paper under soft cheese and acidic fruit to avoid it leaving marks, or wrap clingfilm very tightly around the board.

I like to pop my marble board in the fridge for a couple of hours before serving cheese on it, to ensure the cheeses stay nice and cool. Clean marble with a mixture of equal amounts of washing-up liquid, vinegar and warm water, then rinse with warm water and allow to dry naturally.

Cheese tools

A cheeseboard is nothing without a good cheese knife. Believe it or not, the type of cheese knives you use when enjoying your cheeses can be quite important: using the right knife with the right cheese can make cutting easier and can also help preserve the look, texture and even the taste of your cheese. Here' a quick guide to which knives work best with which cheeses.

Ideally, avoid using the same knife for cutting multiple cheeses, as this can lead to cross-contamination and tainting of the cheeses' individual flavours.

1. PARMESAN KNIFE

The Parmesan knife (also known as a spade knife, tagliarini knife or almond knife) has been used for over a hundred years in Italy. The stout knife has a short handle and a drop-shaped blade which ends with a sharp pointed tip that is purpose-built to break off chunks of hard cheeses. This knife also doubles up as a useful scoring blade for marking and/or breaking the rind of large Parmesan wheels for cutting.

2. FLAT CHEESE KNIFE

This knife resembles a cleaver or chisel. Great for semi-soft and semi-hard cheeses, it should be held vertically over the cheese and pushed down to cut off pieces. You can then use the sharp end to cut the pieces down further. As with the Parmesan knife, it's useful for a board crammed with cheeses and other produce where there isn't much room for manoeuvre.

3. CHEESE SPREADER

This knife has a dull blade and rounded contours and is used for spreading soft and creamy cheeses such as goat's cheese onto breads, biscuits and crackers rather than for cutting. It is also called a spatula knife.

4. PRONGED CHEESE KNIFE

The classic French cheese knife. Versatile, with a pronged tip, it has many uses. First cut a piece of cheese, then pick it up with the prongs for serving or plating. It can be used for a range of cheeses, from soft to hard.

5. SOFT CHEESE KNIFE

This sharp, serrated knife has holes along the blade which help prevent soft and semi-soft cheeses from sticking due to the reduced surface area (this blade is known as an open-work blade). You can use the hole to push a gooey piece off the knife more easily.

6. NARROW-PLANE CHEESE KNIFE

This knife has a rectangular blade and both the long and short sides are sharp. It is suitable for slicing hard and semi-hard cheeses as well as chipping away at hard block cheeses and is used vertically, like the flat cheese knife.

7. CHEESE PLANE

A cheese plane is a useful tool for producing consistently thin, even slices of semi-hard and hard cheeses such as Emmental. To 'shave' the cheese, you pass the plane along the top or side of the surface.

8. CHEESE WIRE

This taut wire is made for cutting delicate soft cheeses without crushing them or spreading them too far.

Other kit for your displays

I always add small jars, bowls and ramekins to my boards to hold jams, dips or items in a brine like cornichons or olives. Using dishes on your board adds a bit of height and sometimes the components benefit from being separated from one another, especially if they are strongly flavoured or runny in texture, such as chutneys or honeys. I also like to serve my cheeseboard with small serving plates. You can even build mini charcuterie boards on cute plates to make everything extra personal.

13

How to cut cheese

On a cheeseboard it's important to cut some of the cheeses, as this will encourage your guests to get started. Here are some easy tips on which cheeses are suitable for cutting, and how to cut them, whether they are in wheels, wedges or blocks.

Cheesemonger Tip

It is considered poor etiquette to cut the tip or 'nose' off a wedge of cheese, because that is considered to be the part that is ripest and therefore has the best flavour.

WHOLE SOFT CHEESES

If they are runny, keep them in their outer containers and unwrap them. Cut away the top of the rind if you are serving them for dipping.

SOFT CHEESE WEDGES

I prefer to keep wedges of soft cheese such as brie whole, as they hold together better and don't run off the plate, but if you want to serve them in slices, cut slices along the long edge of the cheese to make long strips so each piece includes the rind and the tip.

HARD CHEESE WEDGES

Cut semi-hard to hard cheese into wedges along the width edge from the narrowest end towards the rind until you reach at least halfway up the wedge. The top half of the wedge can then be cut into wedges along the length edge.

BLUE CHEESE WEDGES

To cut a blue cheese wedge, start at the centre of the thinnest edge (not the rind edge) and cut slices in a radial pattern from that centre point to achieve triangular cheese pieces that all include some rind and edge (or 'nose').

BLOCKS

To cut a block of cheese, first cut it in half to make two rectangular pieces, then cut the pieces along their width to create slices. The slices can then be cut diagonally into triangles, if you like.

LOGS

Cut cheese logs by slicing them widthways (thickly or thinly, as you wish) to create cheese discs.

WHEELS/ROUNDS

To cut a wheel or round of cheese, first cut it in half to make two manageable pieces (if it is large), then cut cheese triangles, slicing from the rind towards the centre point of the sliced edge of the cheese. If you haven't cut the wheel in half, locate the centre of the cheese wheel/round and cut out from that point like spokes on a wheel.

A note on cheese rinds

Almost all cheese rinds, including those covered in a bloom of mould and/or ash, are edible. The only ones that aren't edible are wax or cloth casings. Cheese rinds often have complex flavours that enhance the enjoyment of the cheese, but you may prefer not to eat them. It's completely up to you. If you don't use the rinds, freeze or refrigerate them and add them to your next pan of soup, risotto or stew – they are a wonderful way to add a rich umami flavour to dishes and you can just scoop them out when the dish is cooked.

How to serve cheese

One of the questions we're frequently asked in the cheese shop is how to serve cheese. One of the key pieces of advice I always give customers is to never serve cheese straight from the fridge. All cheeses are best served at room temperature. If you need to prepare the board (or an arrangement of stacked cheeses such as those on The Birthday Board on page 148) ahead of time, make sure you remove them from the fridge in sufficient time before serving. Cheese is a living organism, so serving it a little warmer, rather than fridge cold, enables us to pick up on its umami characteristics more easily, and we perceive flavours better at temperatures close to our own body temperature.

Get the cheeses out of the fridge 1–2 hours before serving and place them on the plate or board you are planning to present them on. Keep them wrapped if you can – this will stop them drying out as they come to room temperature. Slice cheese as close as possible to the time of serving.

How much cheese do you need?

I'm often asked this, and there are lots of factors at play: what occasion is the cheeseboard for? How hungry are your guests? Is the cheese course being served alongside a main meal or is it the centrepiece? Striking the right balance is key, as you want to offer an abundance of delights but not end up with cut pieces of cheese (and other produce) that go to waste.

Portions will vary depending on if you are serving your cheeseboard alongside other food, how greedy your guests are, and if you would like to restock your board when it starts to run low.

The golden rule, however, is 150g (5½oz) of cheese per person, so bear this in mind before you buy and cut your cheeses.

A small 25cm (10in) board	serves 2–4
A medium 30cm (12in) board	serves 4–6
A medium-large 38cm (15in) board	serves 8–10
A very large 46cm (18in) board	serves 10–12

How to store cheese

Cheeses have a sponge-like quality and will absorb flavours and smells that they are surrounded by so, in an ideal world, it's great to have one of the salad drawers in the fridge dedicated to cheese. If this isn't possible, store them well-wrapped on the top shelf.

Cheesemonger Tip

If you have any leftover pieces of cheese, don't throw them away. Keep them for making toasties, baking gratins, adding to cauliflower cheese, crumbling into salads or onto pizzas.

Types of cheese

You can't create a fabulous cheeseboard without a range of fabulous cheeses, so let's have a look at the types of cheeses out there. Cheeses can be broken down on so many ways – the type of milk they are made with, their flavour, age, texture, type of rind, and so on – but let's keep it simple and break them down into five categories:

Fresh & brined cheese

Fresh cheeses are young, rindless white cheeses whose curds have in most cases not been pressed, and brined cheeses are young cheeses preserved using brine. They have a light, milky, subtle flavour and most are soft in texture with no rind. Some fresh cheeses such as feta and goat's cheese are left to ripen and age, which gives them a tangy, tart flavour. The softer the cheese, the higher the water content and the more perishable it is.

Examples: paneer, mascarpone, cottage cheese, feta, halloumi, mozzarella, ricotta, Selle-sur-Cher, Crottin de Chavignol, Banon

Soft white cheese

These melt-in-the-mouth ripened soft cheeses have to be my favourite type of cheese. I associate them with naughtiness and their creamy richness is such an indulgent treat. They have a buttery mouthfeel and a creamy texture and various types of edible rind, from a velvety white crust to a natural bloom of mould, which forms when the cheese is left to ripen for a month or so. The flavour of soft white cheeses ranges from buttery and sweet to complex and earthy.

Examples: Camembert, Ragstone, Capricorn goat, Brie de Meaux, Tunworth, Camembert, Coeur de Neufchâtel

Semi-soft cheese

This popular category of cheese flies off the shelves in my shop. Semi-soft cheeses are creamy with a bouncy rather than runny texture, and their flavour ranges from sweet, mild and nutty to pungent, meaty and earthy. These cheeses have either a dry rind or a washed rind (meaning the rind of the cheese is dipped in brine during the ageing process). The dry-rind cheeses tend to be firmer than washed-rind cheeses.

Examples: Stinking Bishop, Langres, Munster, Époisses de Bourgogne, Taleggio, Jarlsberg, Fontina, Tomme de Savoie, Monterey Jack, Morbier

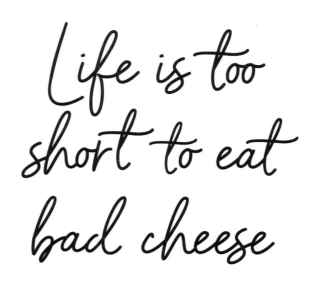

Life is too short to eat bad cheese

Hard cheese

This category includes a wide range of cheeses, from traditional Cheddar to milky Manchego, mature Comté to crumbly 30-month Parmigiano-Reggiano. All hard cheeses are pressed and aged, and the amount of time they are aged for dramatically affects their flavour profiles, with their complexity on the palate increasing and the moisture content decreasing, the longer they are left. The lack of moisture means they have better keeping qualities than soft cheeses.

Examples: Cheddar, Pecorino, Manchego, Gruyère, Caerphilly, Comté, Gouda, Parmesan

Blue cheese

The beautiful veined interior of blue cheeses comes from the way in which they are made, by adding a sprinkle of penicillium mould to the milk before it's curdled to kick off the magical process. Once the cheese is drained and set in moulds, it is then pierced several times which allows the air to penetrate and the blueing to develop. This leads to the formation of mould inside the cheese, and the development of the characteristic flavour facets we associate with blues, a spicy, slightly metallic note that can be assertive, sharp and bitter or subtle and earthy. Texturally, blue cheese varies from creamy and soft to firm and crumbly.

Examples: Gorgonzola, Stilton, Roquefort, Fourme d'Ambert

19

Pairings

Flavour wheel

Cheeses vary widely in flavour depending on the type of milk they are made from, their ripeness, and a range of other factors, so when you're choosing cheeses for your board it can be helpful to consider their flavour profiles, so that you ensure your board offers something for everyone.

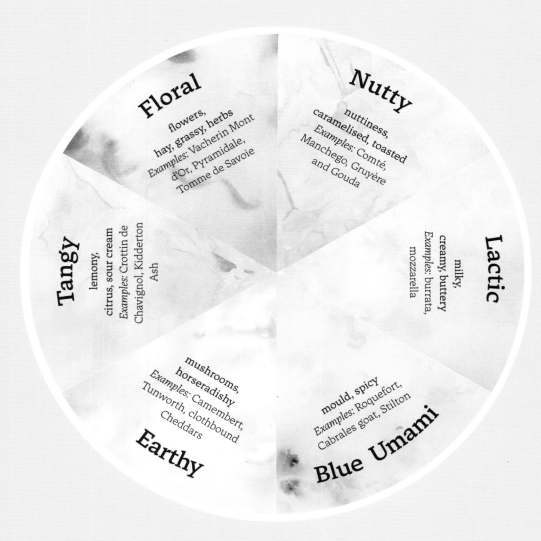

Floral
flowers, hay, grassy, herbs
Examples: Vacherin Mont d'Or, Pyramidale, Tomme de Savoie

Nutty
nuttiness, caramelised, toasted
Examples: Comté, Manchego, Gruyère and Gouda

Tangy
lemony, citrus, sour cream
Examples: Crottin de Chavignol, Kidderton Ash

Lactic
milky, creamy buttery
Examples: burrata, mozzarella

Earthy
mushrooms, horseradishy
Examples: Camembert, Tunworth, clothbound Cheddars

Blue Umami
mould, spicy
Examples: Roquefort, Cabrales goat, Stilton

The science of flavour pairings

When assembling the perfect cheeseboard, it helps to understand how all our senses – not just our sense of taste – inform our perception and help us evaluate what foods are complementary. What we recognize as 'flavour' is not just what our receptors on our tongues pick up (taste), but a fuller sensation that occurs when the olfactory system (sense of smell) and mouthfeel get involved. And our other senses affect how we experience flavour, too.

Sight

The aesthetic impact of a cheeseboard is, of course, key. The colour, texture and arrangement of the components will affect our perception positively or negatively and can make all the difference when it comes to whetting the appetite and giving your guests a sense of eager anticipation.

Taste

The sense of taste has the largest influence on our flavour experience. There are five universally accepted basic tastes that stimulate and are perceived by our taste buds: sweet, salty, sour, bitter and umami.

SWEET

If you, like me, have been burdened (or blessed) with a sweet tooth, you will know that this craving will not subside until you have satisfied it with a sugary treat – for me, this has to be chocolate, which fortunately pairs well with myriad cheeses. Sweetness is often described as the pleasure taste: it is found in simple carbohydrates, notably sugar, which is a core source of energy and hence, is desirable to the human body. A judicious quantity of something sweet – perhaps a drizzle of sweet floral honey, a fruit preserve, chocolate truffles, or some fresh, ripe seasonal fruits – on a cheeseboard is often welcome, countering the saltiness and 'funk' of strong-flavoured cheeses such as a washed-rind Pont L'Evêque or Vacherin and sharp goat's cheeses.

SALTY

The simplest taste receptor in our mouths is the one that detects sodium chloride (salt). Salt is a critical component of the human diet and it enhances the flavour of foods, amplifying sweetness as effectively as it does its savoury notes. Therefore, pairing a salty cured salami or a wider selection of charcuterie with an aged Gouda, for instance, or crispy grilled bacon with a pungent blue, brings out the sweetness of the cheese and simultaneously enhances its umami characteristics. Salty ingredients also work well with young, mild, lactic soft cheeses.

SOUR

Sourness is the perception of acidity in what we consume. The mouth-puckering sensation is common when we eat citrus fruits, pickled foods and foods soured through fermentation. Pairing tart pickles such as piccalilli and pickled cornichons with cheese helps the taste receptors pick up (and balance out) the sweetness of the cheese and balances out the fattiness.

BITTER

Bitter is the most sensitive of the five tastes. Our bodies have an inbuilt wariness of bitter flavours, as bitter compounds are what many plants and other living things produce as a defence mechanism to protect themselves from attack. However, a little bitterness in a food can make it more interesting – consider dark chocolate, or Seville orange marmalade. Bitterness has the potential to work in harmony with a great many cheeses: try shavings of dark chocolate on top of a creamy goat's cheese to create a flavour party on your tongue, a bitter stout with Stilton, or perhaps pickled onion with a chunk of Cheddar.

UMAMI

Known as the 'fifth taste', umami is a deeply savoury deliciousness ('umami' means 'delicious taste' in Japanese) that comes from glutamate, an amino acid that occurs naturally in the human body and in many food and drink products including cured meats, wine, roasted foods, fermented foods such as anchovies, and, of course, cheese. Pairing fresh, mild cheeses with umami-rich ingredients helps boost their savoury tones. A pickled radish may not sound like anything special but the magic it can bring to a cheeseboard is unquestionable – adding this to a washed rind cheese such as Langres, is fantastic: the sharp acid, subtle sweetness and sour aromatics combine with the cheeses' creamy umami and the radish crunch offers the perfect combination of flavours as well as textures.

Smell & aroma

A lot of our customers smell our cheese shop before they see it. Some customers who come into my shop aren't keen on trying certain aged and washed-rind cheeses due to their powerful smell, however it is precisely this characteristic that makes cheese a source of pleasure for others.

The best way to fully appreciate the aroma of a cheese is to bite on it for a few seconds, while holding your breath, with your mouth closed. After a few seconds have passed, exhale through the nose in short bursts. The aroma will reach the olfactory gland, and at this stage you can then pick up on its different nuances.

Cheese has some very unusual characteristics, which have very specific effects in the brain. The combination of taste, texture, feel and aroma create the most incredible sensation.

Touch, texture and mouthfeel (the sensation of foods when they hit our palate and taste receptors) contrubute to our general cheese-eating experience, too, affecting how we receive the flavour on our tongues and evaluate what to pair with the cheese.

Seasonal ingredients

Incorporating fresh seasonal produce when you build your cheeseboard is always a good approach: seasonal produce will not only taste its best, but if you are also serving seasonal cheeses everything is more likely to be complementary on the palate. Here are a few of my favourite seasonal ingredients:

Spring

baby carrots
fresh pesto
new potatoes
radishes
roasted asparagus
young peas in their pods

Autumn

apples
grapes
pears
roasted squash
thyme or rosemary sprigs

Summer

apricots
basil
cherries
fresh berries (strawberries, raspberries, redcurrants, blackcurrants)
fresh figs
heirloom tomatoes or cherry tomatoes
melon
peaches

Winter

blood oranges
celery
clementines
cranberry sauce
pomegranate
rosemary sprigs

Cheese Seasonality

What pasture-fed cows, goats and sheep are eating – and where – affects their milk which, in turn, affects the flavour and texture of the cheese. For example Vacherin, an alpine cheese, is produced using milk from mountain cows grazing on lower pastures during the winter. Milk from the same cows is used to make Comté in the summer, when it is less creamy. Asking your cheesemonger about seasonal cheeses when choosing what you want to put on your cheeseboards encourages you to try something new, and you will also discover what it is that makes a seasonal artisan cheese so unmatched by its mass-produced counterpart.

Pairing cheeses & edible flowers

I love to garnish my cheeseboards with edible flowers. Some cheeseboards benefit from a burst of colour and edible flowers are a perfect way to do that. They can create a true piéce de résistance.

These little beauties are so easy to grow and the seeds are cheap as chips – I have grown edible flowers in my back garden for many years and sell them in my cheese shop. They are also readily available from farmers' markets, local delis, whole food shops or online.

If you can, pick your flowers just before adding them to the board, so they look as vibrant and fresh as possible. If you are storing flowers, keep them in the fridge in a sealed container lined with damp kitchen paper (kitchen towel) and use within a few days.

ROCKET (ARUGULA) FLOWERS: rocket flowers have a peppery, bitter flavour, just like the slender leaves. Perfect with burrata or mozzarella.

CHIVE BLOSSOMS: these have a subtle onion flavour. Use the whole flowers or separate into individual petals. Pair with Cheshire.

HIBISCUS: these flowers are tart and sweet, and an ideal partner for Roquefort.

JASMINE: the white flowers of this climbing plant are intensely fragrant with a strong sweet fragrance and flavour. Pair them with Délice des Crémiers. Note: only *jasmine officinale* flowers are edible.

JOHNNY JUMP UPS: also known as viola, these are a relative of the pansy, and have a mild, lettuce-like vegetal flavour. Serve with soft-ripened goat's milk cheese.

LAVENDER: lavender is part of the mint family and the purple flowers and an assertive, floral and herbaceous flavour that's perfume-y and mildly citrusy. Pair with sweet Gouda.

LEMON VERBENA: the flowers of this plant have a light lemony, slightly herbaceous flavour that works well with Gruyère or Comté.

MARIGOLD: the petals have a mild citrus flavour and slight earthy bitterness and are perfect with Fourme d'Ambert.

NASTURTIUMS: with a mild peppery flavour, these pair beautifully with cheeses like Crottin de Chavignol.

VIOLETS: theses flowers have a sweet, floral flavour and pair brilliantly with Manchego.

Note

Avoid picking flowers in the wild, unless this is permitted and you are 100 per cent positive that what you are picking is edible. Never pull out a plant's roots and do not pick more than a couple of stems from an thriving patch.

Pairing cheeses & herbs

Herbs and cheese are a classic combination, and a handful of herbs adds oodles of visual appeal to a cheeseboard. Herbs arranged on a board with a beautiful selection of cheeses offer an enticing aroma and can function as a flavour pairing, not just a garnish.

When you're considering which herbs to select for your cheeseboard, consider their flavour profiles: generally, the most pungent and strongly-flavoured herbs are suitable companions for strong cheeses, and delicate herbs are better paired with more subtle cheeses.

BASIL: the leaves of this herb have a strong aroma and a rich, warm and spicy flavour with a hint of citrus. The leaves bruise easily, so keep them whole for your board, or incorporate them into a pesto (page 118). Basil is on famously good terms with milky, fresh mozzarella, the sweet, fragrant herb appearing frequently with the cheese in summer months. My summer caprese board wouldn't be complete without these two.

CHIVE: the pretty purple flowers, flower buds and grass-like hollow stalks of this plant all have a mild oniony flavour that pairs well with many cheeses, from spreadable creamy, mild cheeses to soft goat's cheeses.

DILL: dill's delicate, spindly fronds have a mild aniseed flavour and a slight sharpness that peps up a mild creamy cheese such as cottage cheese, spreadable goat's cheese or cream cheese brilliantly. Try pairing it with a fresh Chèvre cheese.

OREGANO: this herb, similar to marjoram, is a member of the mint family. The hardy, pungent leaves have a slightly bitter, sharp taste and it is a familiar aromatic flavour in Greek and Italian cuisines, and Spanish and Latin American food too. The leaves make a good companion for a briny, tangy feta.

ROSEMARY: the leaves of this bushy shrub are powerfully aromatic with aspects of pine and a warm peppery note that pairs well with Pecorino. The sprigs also make a pretty bed for the components of your board. Try infusing honey with a sprig of rosemary by warming the honey with a sprig added to the pan or bowl before drizzling it over a Brie, or incorporate a little rosemary into your favourite biscuit or cracker recipe. The leaves are tough so should be finely chopped if you are serving it to be eaten.

SAGE: This strong, earthy herb with hints of citrus, has velvety leaves and is brilliant paired with strong cheeses: try it with sharp Cheddars – it holds its own with even the most mature candidates. Look out for variegated types of sage, which often have a subtler, less pungent flavour: try pineapple sage or purple sage.

THYME: there are hundreds of varieties of thyme, all with slightly varying flavours, however they all share a common characteristic: a sweet and slightly spicy warmth that is particularly versatile when it comes to cheese. Consider adding a ramekin of thyme honey to your board, scattering a few thyme leaves over cheese biscuits, grilling goat's cheese with thyme sprigs. Or, perhaps, pair it with a rich gorgonzola.

26

Pairing cheeses & wines

Cheese and wine single-handily got me through the 2020 lockdown. My year was made better by trying to keep life at home as normal as can be and throwing a cheese and wine party on Friday nights. We would gather on a Zoom call and talk through our weekly favourite cheese.

In more normal times, one of the questions that I often get asked is, 'what wine should I serve with my cheeseboard?' It is super easy if you follow a few basic rules. Here is my simple guide to help you achieve a perfect wine-and-cheese combination.

Everything is fine if you have cheese & wine

If they grow together, they go together

Both cheese and wine are produced as a way of preserving nature's bounty, so it makes sense to match wines and cheeses from regions that share a similar topography. For instance, a crisp Sauvignon Blanc from the Loire Valley is a perfect match for a tangy, lemony Sainte-Maure de Touraine: the wine comes from the same region as the cheese and it shares similar fresh, acidic characteristics.

White wines for a win

As a rule, I tend to think white wines match a wider variety of cheeses than red wines, as reds have a tendency to overpower cheese. Be wary of heavily oaked whites, however.

Bring on the bubbles

If in doubt, pop open some bubbles. The bubbles in Champagne or sparkling wines work to strip the fat off your palette, making the next bite even more sensational.

Try Champagne with a creamy cheese like Delice de Bourgogne. Other soft cheeses as Brie, Muenster, Camembert, Chaource, Tunworth or Époisses work well, too. And Parmesan and Prosecco are of course a match made in heaven.

Sweet & smelly

Washed-rind cheeses like Époisses and Stinking Bishop, and crumbly, pungent Blues, work really well with rich, sweet and/or fortified wines such as Port and Sauternes or a spicy Gewürztraminer.

Note
The harder and more complex the cheese, the better it can cope with big, bold tannins in wine.

27

Match the strengths

Pair wines and cheeses that are equal in intensity: you don't want a strong, highly tannic wine such as Cabernet Sauvignon with a subtle youthful cheese, as the wine will overwhelm it. Choose a wine that allows the nuances of the cheese to come through and not be outshone, perhaps a delicate Pinot Noir or Chenin Blanc. The harder and more aged the cheese, the richer the wine can be. There really isn't anything better than a well-aged cheese, apart from when you pair it with the perfect wine – for strong, complex cheeses you can crack open a robust red, perhaps a Shiraz or Rhone wine.

Choose your red wine carefully

Match heavy reds with heavy tasting strong cheese e.g Big bold reds / Port go well with strong blues like Stilton.

Cheese & rosé all day

Rosé is the perfect accompaniment for cheese. Dry styles (such as a light Provençal rosé) complement almost all cheese, especially fresh, young cheeses.

A few pairing suggestions

BLUE CHEESES:
Amontillado sherry
Ruby Port

GOAT'S CHEESES:
Pinot Gris
Sauvignon Blanc

MILD, YOUNG, SOFT CHEESES
e.g. mozzarella, ricotta:
Pinot Grigio
Riesling (sweet or dry)

SALTY CHEESES
e.g. feta, mature Cheddar:
Beaujolais
Chardonnay
Malbec
Merlot

SWEET AND NUTTY CHEESES
e.g. Jarlsberg, Comté:
Chardonnay
Rioja

SOFT, PUNGENT CHEESES
e.g. Brie de Meaux:
Gewürztraminer
Pinot Noir

If you like it, you can't go wrong

Pairing guidelines are exactly that: a guide. If you enjoy a certain cheese and wine, that makes it RIGHT! Your taste buds are truly your best guide and even the most unlikely pairings will delight some cheese lovers.

Other drinks pairings

Consider exploring other alcoholic beverages when you serve a cheeseboard. A dry cider pairs well with mature Cheddar, and a rich, dark porter is an excellent companion for Gruyère. For non-alcoholic cheese-pairings, try elderflower cordial with chèvre or apple juice with mature Cheddar.

Pairing cheeses & meat

Cheese and meat, particularly charcuterie, are a match made in heaven but, like many other pairings, certain meats and cheese complement each other better than others. Here are some of my favourite combinations which will guarantee your charcuterie and cheeseboard has that wow factor.

Prosciutto & Parmesan

You can't go wrong with a salty and sweet pairing and these two big-hitters pack a powerful punch. Parmesan, with its salt crystals and crumbly texture, pairs beautifully with buttery-rich, soft prosciutto.

Salami & Gouda

Salami is a time-honoured crowdpleaser and a foolproof pairing for many different types of cheese, particularly semi-soft cheeses such as Gouda. I love Old Amsterdam in particular, as it has a beautiful sweetness and fudge-like flavour which is stunning with the spicy, sweet, savoury flavours of the salami. Try salami with Pecorino too – it encourages the subtle, sweet and smoky flavours of Pecorino to emerge on the palate and the meat's smokiness rounds out the smooth sweetness of the Pecorino.

'Nduja & Comté

'Nduja is a soft, spreadable pork product from Calabria flavoured with chilli that will definitely add a kick to your cheese feast. Rich, creamy and nutty cheese such as Comté and Alpine cheeses are a delicious partner for 'nduja, balancing out the spicy heat with their creamy texture and mouthfeel.

Jamón Iberico & Stilton

The rich, saltiness of Stilton works so well with the Jamón Iberico. The sweet and sour flavours of the meat and cheese complement each other perfectly, with the jamón adding an earthy undertone to the pairing.

Pairing cheese with fish

It's often thought that cheese and fish don't belong together however, a carefully selected pairing can enhance the flavour of your cheese. For example, cream cheese and smoked salmon are a classic combination.

'Nduja & Comté

Jamón Iberico & Stilton

Salami & Gouda

Prosciutto & Parmesan

How to Build the Perfect Cheeseboard:
the cheat sheet

These simple step-by-step instructions show you how to assemble a cheeseboard from start to finish. Each element brings diversity in flavour, texture and visual appeal. Of course, these elements and my recommendations are just guidelines. If you don't fancy a blue cheese or salami on your board, just change it up as you prefer. These boards are a form of self-expression, so if you love it, use it!

Let's start with the cheese, the main event – the reason a cheeseboard is a cheeseboard.

Step 1: Select your cheese

a) Aim for variety in the type of milk, age and texture, as well as in shape and colour, or stick to one and make it star of the show (a whole baked feta perhaps, or baked Camembert).

b) Decide on your taste preference:

Fresh, mild & creamy, sweet
burrata, Comté / Gruyère

Buttery, rich, sharp & complex
Brie

Smooth & nutty, salty & smelly
aged Gouda, aged Cheddar, Parmigiano Reggiano

Caramel crunchy
Manchego / Basques

Earthy & robust
blue cheese

Step 2: Pick your meat or fish (optional)

- prosciutto
- bacon or pancetta
- bresaola
- jamón/ Ibérico ham
- chorizo
- 'nduja
- ham or coppa
- saucisson or salami
- cooked sausages
- cold roast meats
- sausage rolls
- smoked salmon
- cooked prawns
- anchovy fillets

Step 3: Pick your fresh fruit & veggies

Fresh seasonal fruit and vegetables complement the saltiness of the cheese. (See the seasonal lists on page 23.)

Step 4: Pick your accompaniments

- runny honey or honeycomb
- chocolate
- dried fruit: *dried figs, dried apricots, dried cranberries, sun-dried tomatoes*
- pickles, preserves and condiments: *piccalilli, cornichons, gherkins, pickled onions, capers, chutneys, quince jelly or paste, onion marmalade, jams, relishes, balsamic glaze, olives*

- Nuts (smoked, unsalted or salted, roasted, as you prefer): *pine nuts, walnuts, cashews, honey-roasted peanuts, walnuts, Marcona almonds, toasted hazelnuts, pistachios, pecans*
- dips and deli items: *pesto, hummus, marinated artichoke hearts*

Step 5: Pick your bread or crackers

- ciabatta
- French stick/baguette
- bread rolls
- rye bread
- water biscuits
- cheese crackers: *cheese/fennel, rosemary, fig, etc.*

- sourdough
- crostini
- oat biscuits/oatcakes
- grissini/breadsticks
- crispbreads

Step 6: Pick your herb &/or flower garnish

Use the cheeses and other components of your board to inform your choice of garnishes. (Follow the guide on pages 24–26 for notes on flavour profiles.)

- basil
- chives
- dill
- hibiscus
- jasmine

- lavender
- lemon verbena
- nasturtiums
- rosemary

Everyday Cheeseboard

This is my everyday, super-easy cheeseboard. You can use whatever you have to hand in the fridge or local shop and create a stunning centrepiece that is guaranteed to impress. Whether it is for a starter, main course, dessert or even an indulgent snack, the beauty of being able to assemble a board like this is it will work for any occasion and shouldn't take much effort at all.

Step 1:
Assemble

Once you have chosen your board (I use a round wooden one as it gives a lot of room to play around with the set-up), start organizing the things that take up the most room on the board, such as ramekins, dishes and/or small bowls (keep them empty for now). This is a great way of planning the board, adding some height to the presentation and preparing ahead of time.

Step 2:
THE CHEESE

The main event and the star of the show! Take the cheese out of the fridge and place it on the board a few hours before serving so it has a chance to reach room temperature.

I like to serve a hard cheese, a blue cheese and a soft cheese or goat's cheese, a combination of fresh, smelly and aged: this makes for a perfect range of flavours and textures for your cheeseboard. For this board I've used Montgomery Cheddar, Cornish Blue and Camembert.

I like to keep the soft cheese and goat's cheese whole as they stay in better condition this way and the soft cheese won't ooze onto the board. Cut the hard cheese into slices or cubes just before serving and stack them up – this makes it easier for guests to grab a piece and makes the board look more interesting.

Step 3:
THE CHARCUTERIE

Only a basic deli salami has been used here. You can add your meats a few different ways: in a simple stack (this saves time if you're in a rush), fanned out in a line or half-circle (this works best on large boards since it takes up more space) or by folding larger pieces into fun shapes (this adds some visual interest). For this cheese plate, I opted to fold our charcuterie pieces since there was a lot to get onto the board.

Step 4:
THE CRACKERS OR BREAD

Don't go overboard on this. You want to give as much room as possible to the cheese. Just a handful of crackers, biscuits or crostini on the board is ample for some crunch, especially when

34

you have additional accompaniments such as meat, fruit and/or vegetables. Set out a bowl of extra crackers for those who want them. Fan your selected bread/crackers out along the edges of the board to make them easy to grab. I used rosemary crackers here.

Now we have our main components on the board, it is time to have some fun with it and fill in those gaps. This is where the cheeseboard really starts to come together and where you get to give it the WOW factor.

Step 5:
THE ACCOMPANIMENTS

First, add some fruit and vegetables. I used strawberries, raspberries, sliced apples and cherry tomatoes here, but you can use any fruit or vegetables you have to hand. Keep it seasonal if you can (page 23). If the fruit isn't bite sized, I like to break some or all of it into relatively small pieces and scatter it in a few places across the board – I placed the fruit around the outside of the board to help it look balanced.

Next, add the nuts if you're using them. Drop a few nuts into the smaller blank spaces on the middle of your board to add some texture and

cover any open spots. Leave a few spaces around the edges for any extras you're adding!

Next, fill those ramekins, dishes and/or bowls. You can add anything you like to these little bowls – olives, nuts, more fruit, preserves, pickles, etc. This board has pots of honey, olives and cornichons with silverskin pickled onions; all are easy storecupboard essentials. Other favourites include pesto (page 118), high-quality salted butter, fig or blackberry jam, beetroot (beet) hummus (page 163) and flaked sea salt.

Step 6:
THE GARNISH

You are almost ready to serve your cheeseboard. All that's left is to fill in any remaining gaps to make your board look full and inviting. I always go for something green to help break up the colour, since otherwise the display can lean a little too far into the yellows, whites and browns. Herbs like rosemary, thyme, dill and

basil add an incredible aroma as well as looking beautiful. As a finishing touch, edible flowers bring some more colour, aroma and taste to the cheeseboard. I've used rosemary here, as it was growing in my garden and it adds some welcome pepperiness.

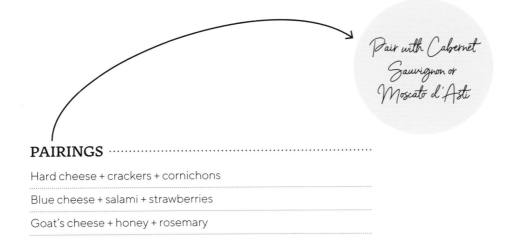

Pair with Cabernet Sauvignon or Moscato d'Asti

PAIRINGS ·····························

Hard cheese + crackers + cornichons

Blue cheese + salami + strawberries

Goat's cheese + honey + rosemary

EVERYDAY
BOARDS

The Timeless Classics

This board is a homage to fromage. For this timeless classic selection, I am featuring our four iconic best-selling cheeses. Brie de Meaux, the most famous French cheese, is known for its rich creamy flavour, which makes it a perfect pair for our salty and sharp Montgomery Cheddar. A Colston Bassett Stilton is a semi-soft salty blue, and to finish we have the Sainte-Maure de Touraine goat's cheese, a young cheese with citrus notes. To bring out the best in these cheeses, we've created a spread of savoury sides, including piccalilli and fig relish.

COMPONENTS

Cheese
250g (9oz) Montgomery Cheddar
250g (9oz) Colston Bassett
   Stilton
200g (7oz) Sainte-Maure de
   Touraine (1 log)
250g (9oz) Brie de Meaux

Accompaniments
1 pear
2 celery sticks
bunch of red grapes
handful of walnuts
50g (1¾oz) fig relish
50g (1¾oz) My Perfect
   Piccalilli (page 160)

Bread and crackers
100g (3½oz) wafer cheese
   crackers

Garnish
50g (1¾oz) pea shoots or
   microgreens

PREP

Slice the Cheddar into long batons. Crumble the Stilton into chunks. Slice the Sainte-Maure de Touraine log into equal rounds. Finely slice the pear and cut the celery into batons.

ASSEMBLE

Keep the Brie whole and place it on the bottom left corner of the board, pointing in. Place one small empty ramekins in the centre of the board and one larger ramekin in the top left corner. On either side of the board, place the Cheddar and Stilton, criss-crossing the Cheddar batons. Place the celery batons and grapes between the Brie and the Sainte-Maure de Touraine at the bottom of the board. Scatter the walnuts between the Brie and the Stilton then fan the crackers out along the board so that they form a line between the two ramekins. Fill the top of the board with sliced pear. Fill the small ramekin with fig relish and the larger one with piccalilli, respectively. Garnish the board with the pea shoots or microgreens.

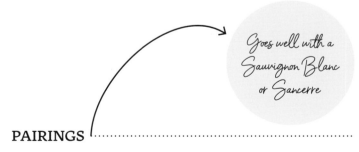

Goes well with a Sauvignon Blanc or Sancerre

PAIRINGS

Montgomery Cheddar + celery + piccalilli

Stilton + walnut + fig relish

Sainte-Maure + grapes + pea shoots or microgreen sprouts

Brie + pear

Brunch Board

Brunch happens to be one of my favourite meals. Whether it is a boozy girls' gathering or knocking up something special for guests we are hosting, I can't think of a better way to start my day than a sharing a cheese brunch board. You can sit for hours grazing away, building amazing flavour combinations.

The Mimosa is a perfect blend of Prosecco and orange juice and is my favourite brunch drink. The zingy, fresh hit of orange and the cool crisp bubbles are the perfect pairing for salty bacon and soft cheese. A Bloody Mary also accompanies cheese well: the tomato juice, Worcestershire sauce and hot sauce, with celery and olives to garnish, have a tartness that works really well with this board.

COMPONENTS

Cheese
180g (6¼oz) full-fat cream
  cheese
200g (7oz) Brie

Meat and fish
10 slices of streaky bacon
200g (7oz) sliced smoked salmon

Accompaniments
1 cucumber
40g (1½oz) radishes
½ lemon
1 ripe avocado
2 soft-boiled eggs
100g (3½oz) Hot Peach Pickle
  (page 161)
30g (1oz) honey
15 mixed cherry tomatoes

For the bagel seasoning
1 tsp dried garlic
1 tsp dried onion
1 tsp poppy seeds
1 tsp toasted sesame seeds
2 tsp flaked sea salt

For the pickled red onion
1 red onion
2 tbsp white wine vinegar
1 tbsp caster (superfine) sugar
1 tbsp flaked sea salt

Bread and crackers
5 bagels

Garnish
4 dill sprigs

Mimosa or Bloody Mary (or both)

PAIRINGS

Cream cheese + smoked salmon + dill + lemon

Cream cheese + pickled onion + bagel seasoning + cucumber

Brie + tomato + streaky bacon + egg + avocado

PREP

Make the bagel seasoning
Stir the ingredients together in a small bowl.

Make the pickled red onions
Thinly slicing the red onion using a mandoline. Place it in a bowl and add the vinegar, sugar, salt and 4 teaspoons of water. Set aside to marinate for 2 hours before serving, then drain off half of the pickling liquid.

Fry the bacon in a frying pan (skillet) over a medium heat until crisp. Drain on kitchen paper.

Thinly slice the cucumber. Halve one of the radishes, leave one whole, and thinly slice the rest. Thinly slice the lemon and halve, stone and thinly slice the avocado.

Shell and halve the eggs. Put the drained pickled onion in a ramekin and the peach pickle in another small bowl. Pour the honey into a small glass jar and add a honey drizzler, and put the cream cheese in a bowl.

ASSEMBLE

With the short end of the board facing you (the handle at the furthest end), place the Brie on the centre-left of the board. Place the bowl of cream cheese at the top right of the board and the honey, bagel seasoning and pickle bowls or ramekins a third of the way up the board, with the pickled red onions in the bottom right corner. Arrange the bagels down the centre of the board. Arrange the halved eggs along the bottom of the board with the bacon and avocado fanned out next to them. Fold the smoked salmon slices loosely and arrange them near the bowl of cream cheese, along with the cucumber slices. Place the tomatoes to the left of the Brie and place the radishes near the pickle. Fill the gaps on the board with the lemon slices and garnish the board with dill.

Perfect Summer Picnic

This is the ideal cheeseboard that you can pack up and take away for any occasion. Sunshine, good cheese, great wine, friends, the great outdoors and picnic blankets – what could be better than that? Us Brits love a picnic, and this cheeseboard is full of some picnic classics. Keep things simple with homemade pressed picnic sandwiches and a seasonal potato salad or you could even go all out and make your own Scotch eggs and sausage rolls. Plus, it's the perfect opportunity to make good use of some seasonal favourites.

COMPONENTS

Cheese
125g (4½oz) mozzarella ball, thickly sliced
10 mozzarella bocconcini
250g (9oz) Comté
200g (7oz) mature Cheddar
200g (7oz) Brie

Meat
8 slices of prosciutto
4 mini Scotch eggs
5 slices of ham
6 mini sausage rolls

Accompaniments
100g (3½oz) celery sticks
100g (3½oz) carrots
100g (3½oz) cucumber
50g (1¾oz) feta-stuffed red peppers
3 shop-bought spicy prawn skewers
100g (3½oz) Hot Honey (page 165)
200g (7oz) hummus
small bunch of red grapes
handful of sea salt crisps

For the pressed picnic sandwich
1 loaf of focaccia
40g (1½oz) pesto
2 cooked chicken breasts, sliced
10 slices of salami
40g (1½oz) sun-dried tomatoes, finely chopped
20g (¾oz) pitted olives, drained and finely chopped
50g (1¾oz) roasted red (bell) peppers from a jar, finely chopped

For the potato salad
200g (7oz) new potatoes
1 red onion, thinly sliced
2 tbsp red wine vinegar
20g (¾oz) cornichons, thinly sliced
40g (1½oz) mixed cooked green beans and peas
10g (⅓oz) fresh dill, finely chopped
olive oil, for drizzling

Bread and crackers
100g (3½oz) sourdough crackers

Garnish
handful of basil
handful of edible flowers

PREP

Make the pressed picnic sandwich

Cut the focaccia in half lengthways, spread the pesto on both halves, then begin to layer your ingredients on the bottom half, starting with the cooked chicken breast and salami. Scatter over the chopped sun-dried tomatoes, olives and peppers all over the layer, then evenly place the mozzarella slices all over the bottom half. Place the top half of the focaccia on top and wrap the whole loaf in greaseproof paper then cling film (plastic wrap).

Put the sandwich on a chopping board, place some heavy books on top, then put into the fridge for 12 hours.

After 12 hours, unwrap the sandwiches and slice into squares for serving. Wrap tightly in fresh greaseproof paper and tie with string to keep it intact.

Make the potato salad

Cook the new potatoes in a pan of boiling water for about 10 minutes until tender. Drain and leave to cool, then pop the sliced onion into a small bowl, add the red wine vinegar then add the potatoes, cornichons, green beans and peas and dill. Drizzle with olive oil and mix well.

Place the bocconcini mozzarella balls, prosciutto and basil onto cocktail sticks to create mini cheese skewers.

Halve 3 of the mini Scotch eggs.

Cut the celery and carrots into batons. Slice the cucumber into rounds.

Cut the Comté into cubes and slice the Cheddar and Brie into triangles.

ASSEMBLE

Place the Brie slices arranged in a circle on the central right of the board and the Comté on the bottom-right of the board. Place the feta-stuffed peppers in a small dish on the bottom left corner of the board and fan the Cheddar slices around the dish. Fill the ramekins with hot honey and hummus and place in the centre of the board. Lay the grapes above the ramekin of hummus and the vegetable crudites between the hummus and the Brie. Place the sandwiches in the top right corner and the ham below the Brie. Place the bowl of potato salad directly below the sandwiches. Arrange the mini Scotch eggs, sausage rolls, mini cheese skewers and spicy prawn skewers all over the board. Fill in the gaps with crisps and cucumber. Garnish with the edible flowers.

Pairs well with a sweet rose or lemonade

PAIRINGS

Mozzarella + ham + basil + feta-stuffed red pepper
Comté + celery + hot honey
Cheddar + crisps + hot honey
Brie + potato salad + ham

Cosy Night In

If a night at home with delicious cheese and good wine sounds like your vibe, this is the selection for you. To be enjoyed with loved ones, there is something wonderful about sharing this board in front of a fire and having a good catch-up. This is a simple cheeseboard with some fruity accompaniments paired with a selection of wines, but if you just wanted to serve one white and one red, opt for the Pinot Noir and the Riesling.

COMPONENTS

Cheese
100g (3½oz) fresh Chèvre log
200g (7oz) Gouda
200g (7oz) Gruyère
150g (5½oz) Gorgonzola Dolce
200g (7oz) Brie

Accompaniments
1 red apple
100g (3½oz) red grapes
50g (1¾oz) strawberries
50g (1¾oz) shelled pistachios
50g (1¾oz) blueberries
50g (1¾oz) shop-bought red (bell)
   pepper chutney

Bread and crackers
handful of light water biscuits

Garnish
2 thyme sprigs

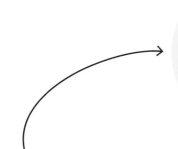

Try Chenin Blanc, Shiraz, Riesling, Chardonnay or Pinot Noir

PREP

Cut a few slices of the goat's cheese log, cut the Gouda into long, pointed triangles, the Gruyère into batons and the Gorgonzola into cubes. Keep the Brie whole.

Cut the apple into thin slices and halve the grapes and strawberries.

ASSEMBLE

Starting from the top left, place the cheeses on the board in the following order, Gouda, Brie, Gorgonzola, Gruyère and goat's cheese. Be sure to leave a gap between each cheese.

The triangles of Gouda and Brie should point towards the centre.

Next, fill the gaps between the cheeses. Place the sprigs of thyme between the Gouda and Brie then scatter the pistachios in the gap between the Brie and Gorgonzola. Pile the strawberries in the space between the Gorgonzola and Gruyère and lay the apple at the bottom of the board between the goat's cheese and Gruyère. Place the grape halves between the goat's cheese and Gouda. Sprinkle the blueberries in the empty spaces on the bottom half of the board.

Place the red pepper chutney in a small ramekin and serve alongside the board with the water biscuits. Garnish with the thyme.

PAIRINGS

Chèvre + pistachios + Chenin Blanc

Gouda + apple + Pinot Noir

Gruyère + red (bell) pepper chutney + Chardonnay

Gorgonzola Dolce + grapes + Riesling

Brie + strawberries + blueberries + Shiraz

Farmers' Market

Few things in life bring me as much joy as a Sunday at the farmers' market. The vibrant colours, the delicious aromas, and don't get me started on the cheese! It's a place to feel joyful, to unwind and restore. This board is all about celebrating the seasons; full of fresh flavours and colours. Take advantage of the natural beautiful state the veggies are in when they come straight from the farm, and the connection with the farmer who made that delicious buffalo mozzarella you love so much. Combining soft Délice de Bourgogne with tangy soured cream and mayonnaise creates a delicious creamy dip for the vegetables. The vegetables used here are ideal for a springtime gathering but you could substitute these for whatever is in season and enjoy the board all year round.

COMPONENTS

Cheese
250g (9oz) Délice de Bourgogne, at room temperature
250g (9oz) buffalo mozzarella ball

Accompaniments
6 asparagus spears
40g (1½oz) young peas in their pods
100g (3½oz) cherry tomatoes
100g (3½oz) plum tomatoes on the vine
5 baby carrots with tops intact
50g (1¾oz) purple sprouting broccoli
4 baby cucumbers
100g (3½oz) beetroot (beets) or watermelon radishes

For the Délice dip
4 tbsp soured cream
1 tbsp mayonnaise
bunch of spring onions (scallions), finely sliced
bunch of parsley, finely chopped
bunch of dill, broken into small fronds

Bread and crackers
100g (3½oz) rosemary Linguette

Garnish
3 spring onions (scallions)
handful of dill
basil leaves

PREP

Make the Délice dip
Mix the Délice de Bourgogne with the soured cream and mayonnaise in a bowl until well combined, then add the spring onions (scallions) and the chopped parsley and dill.

Blanch the asparagus spears in boiling water for 5 minutes then drain and chill in iced water. Drain again once cool.
   Gently open the pods of about half of the young peas, halve a handful of the cherry tomatoes, peel the carrots (leaving the tops on), and break the purple sprouting broccoli into florets. Quarter the baby cucumbers lengthways. Using a mandolin, finely slice the raw beetroot (beets) or watermelon radishes.

ASSEMBLE

Place a large ramekin of Délice cheese dip and a small ramekin with the buffalo mozzarella in the centre of the board, leaving around 10cm (4in) between the two dishes. Make a pile of asparagus and purple sprouting broccoli in the lower right corner of the board. Fan the beetroot or radishes around the right side of the ramekin of Délice dip and add the carrots to the central right side of the board. Pour the tomatoes into the top left corner of the board then lay the young pea pods and cucumber quarters below them, on the left of the ramekin of Délice dip. On either side of the ramekins, make two small piles of the Linguette. Garnish with whole spring onions (scallions) and the fronds of dill. Place the basil on top of the buffalo mozzarella.

PAIRINGS

Délice de Bourgogne + tomato + young peas

Délice de Bourgogne + cucumber

Délice de Bourgogne + carrots + dill

Délice de Bourgogne + purple sprouting broccoli

Mozzarella + asparagus + basil

Goes well with light reds like Gamay

Fruit Pairing Cheeseboard

The beauty of making a fruit and cheese platter is that you get to customise it with all of your favourite fruits and cheeses. Use what you have to hand, what's in season or even what you are growing in your garden – the sky is the limit as to what you put on your board. Perfect fruit and cheese pairing can create an epic cheeseboard, a pairing such as Brie, pear and champagne makes entertaining so easy and delicious.

COMPONENTS

Cheese
200g (7oz) Pecorino
200g (7oz) aged Gouda
150g (5½oz) mini Brie
200g (7oz) Fourme d'Ambert

Accompaniments
½ pear
1 passion fruit
40g (1½oz) cherry tomatoes
4 strawberries

1 peach
2 tbsp wildflower honey
handful of dried apricots
handful of dried cranberries
handful of walnuts
30g (1oz) black grapes
1 tbsp almonds
4 physalis (cape gooseberries)

Bread and crackers
40g (1½oz) water biscuits

PREP

Cut the pear into thin slices. Halve the passion fruit, the cherry tomatoes and two of the strawberries. Cut the peach into thin wedges.

Cut the Pecorino into long pointed triangles and crumble half of the aged Gouda into rough chunks.

ASSEMBLE

Place a ramekin in the centre of the board and fill it with the honey. Sit the Brie above the ramekin and drizzle with some of the honey. Make a pile of aged Gouda in the upper right-hand corner of the board and scatter the dried apricots and cranberries next to it. Place the passion fruit halves in the top left and bottom right corners of the board. Fan the pile of Pecorino triangles from the centre of the board to the bottom left corner then sit the Fourme d'Ambert on the left of the board, leaving some room between the cheeses.

Fan the water biscuits from the centre of the board to the bottom right corner then add the pear slices alongside them. Pile the walnuts in the top left corner above the cheeses. Lay the grapes along the bottom of the board. Fill any gaps with the strawberries, peaches, cherry tomatoes, almonds and physalis (cape gooseberries).

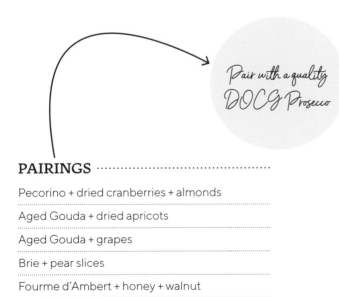

Pair with a quality DOCG Prosecco

PAIRINGS

Pecorino + dried cranberries + almonds

Aged Gouda + dried apricots

Aged Gouda + grapes

Brie + pear slices

Fourme d'Ambert + honey + walnut

Whisky Cheeseboard

Board Style: Ceramic plate
Serves: 2

Stock up your drinks cabinet and dive into this beautiful selection of cheeses paired with our potent whisky and bourbon favourites. We've chosen four bold cheeses that can stand up to a serious drink, including the award-winning Winslade, plus a handful of bold bites that pack a bright hit of flavour. This simple and delicious board is perfect for cheese and whisky lovers alike.

COMPONENTS

Cheese
200g (7oz) Shropshire Blue
130g (4½oz) Banon
250g (9oz) Winslade
200g (7oz) Appenzeller

Meat
100g (3½oz) sliced salami

Accompaniments
2 fresh apricots
20g (¾oz) cornichons
handful of spicy almonds
20g (¾oz) small pickled onions

Bread and crackers
small loaf crusty bread

Garnishes
lavender sprigs
thyme sprigs

PREP

Crumble half of the Shropshire Blue into small chunks. Unwrap the Banon cheese, leaving it in the chestnut leaves. Remove part of the top of the Winslade by making a cut around the rind on one side, creating an open side for dipping. Cut the Appenzeller into long triangle shards. Slice the loaf of bread into 5mm (¼-in) thick pieces, and toast. Halve the apricots and cut two of the halves into thin wedges. Place the cornichons in a ramekin.

ASSEMBLE

Arrange the chunks of Shropshire Blue on a round board with the remaining half intact. Add toasts in small piles. Fan out the Appenzeller triangles and place the Winslade and Banon, leaving some room between them. Fill the gaps with almonds, apricots, cornichons, salami and pickled onions, and place a small spoon into the Winslade for scooping out the cheese. Garnish the Banon with lavender and thyme sprigs.

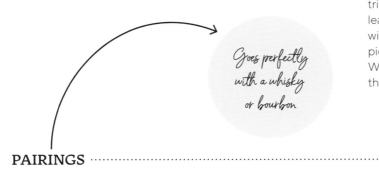

Goes perfectly with a whisky or bourbon

PAIRINGS

Shropshire Blue + apricots + Woodford Reserve bourbon

Banon + salami + single malt light and sweet whisky

Winslade + almonds + Jim Beam Black bourbon

Appenzeller + cornichons +12-year-old Glenrothes Single Malt whisky

Mezze Platter

Mezze is a light meal made up of a variety of small dishes which can include dips, vegetables, cheeses and meats. This is my go-to meal out in north London on a Friday night, so here is my mezze-inspired cheeseboard: a little bit of everything tucked into a delicious platter, meant to be enjoyed together. This board uses a lot of deli favourites, so it comes together very quickly. The cheeses here are all very firm and very salty, so they make a wonderful match to the Sauvignon Blanc or Riesling.

Wine and mezze is a must. A light-bodied white wine with citrus notes like Sauvignon Blanc is a wonderful accompaniment to salty saganaki as it brings out the natural sweetness and it also pairs well with the nutty flavour of hummus.

COMPONENTS

Cheese
150g (5½oz) saganaki
200g (7oz) halloumi

Accompaniments
½ lemon
20g (¾oz) runny honey
4 radishes
3 roasted red (bell) peppers
4 small cucumbers
2 carrots
handful of cherry tomatoes
3 large fresh figs
4 dried figs
200g (7oz) tzatziki
150g (5½oz) tabbouleh
200g (7oz) baba ganoush

200g (7oz) hummus
400g (14oz) roasted chickpeas
  (page 131)
6 dolmas (stuffed grape leaves)
handful of mixed nuts
50g (1¾oz) mixed olives
extra-virgin olive oil, for drizzling

Bread and crackers
3 pitta breads

Garnish
2 sprigs of thyme

PREP

Slice the saganaki and halloumi. Fry the saganaki in a frying pan (skillet) over a gentle heat then put it in a small serving dish with a squeeze of lemon juice and drizzle of honey. Grill the halloumi on a griddle pan over a medium heat for a few minutes until golden brown then add it to the dish with the saganaki.

Slice the pitta into bite-sized triangles, thinly slice the radishes, red (bell) peppers and cucumber, and cut the carrots into batons. Halve the cherry tomatoes, quarter or halve the fresh and dried figs, and put the tzatziki, tabbouleh and baba ganoush into three separate small bowls or ramekins. Slice the lemon and put the honey in a small jar.

ASSEMBLE

Place the dish of saganaki and halloumi on a large board and add the hummus to the dish, topping it with a few of the roasted chickpeas. Put the small bowls or ramekins of dips and tabbouleh around the board. Add the rest of the ingredients on the board around the ramekins or bowls. Lightly drizzle olive oil over the baba ganoush and garnish the cheese with the thyme. There is nothing better to dip into hummus than pillowy-soft pitta bread!

Pair with a Sauvignon Blanc or Riesling

PAIRINGS

Saganaki + honey + thyme + fresh figs

Saganaki + tzatziki + tabbouleh

Halloumi + hummus

Halloumi + dolmas + dried figs

Après Ski Board

Inspired by the French Alps and my best memories of eating amazing mountain cheeses next to an open fire, this spread is guaranteed to transport you to a five-star ski lodge. This deluxe snacking platter has a rustic edge that's made for some sweet post-skiing indulgence, so come in from the cold and dig into our selection of rich, aromatic cheeses including a fruity, funky 36-month aged Comté and spoonable truffle fondue, plus some bites for easy, cheesy dipping and snacking like crunchy cornichons, mini saucisson, baguette, and more.

COMPONENTS

Cheese
300g (10½oz) 36-month aged
    Comté
300g (10½oz) Gruyère
400g (14oz) Emmental
250g (9oz) Beaufort
250g (9oz) Bleu d'Auvergne

Meat
15 mini Herbes de Provence
    saucissons
100g (3½oz) sliced prosciutto

Accompaniments
200g (7oz) new potatoes
1 cauliflower
1 apple of your choice
50g (1¾oz) cornichons
handful of cherries
2 bunches of redcurrants

For the truffle fondue
1 garlic clove
400ml (14fl oz/1⅔ cups) white
    wine
juice of ½ lemon
3 tsp cornflour (cornstarch)
1 tsp truffle paste
small drop of truffle oil
pinch of freshly grated nutmeg
10g (¼oz) fresh black truffle
freshly ground black pepper

Bread and crackers
1 small crusty French baguette

Garnish
bunch of rosemary
bunch of thyme

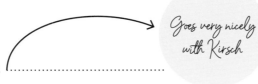

Goes very nicely with Kirsch

PAIRINGS

Truffle fondue + crusty bread + cornichons

Truffle fondue + cauliflower

Truffle fondue + saucisson + apple

Beaufort + cherries

Beaufort + saucisson + cornichons

PREP

Make the truffle fondue
Begin by grating the Comté, Gruyère and 300g (10½oz) of the Emmental. Next, place a fondue pan over a low heat and rub a garlic clove on the base of the pan. Increase the heat to medium, then add the wine and lemon juice. Bring to the boil then add the grated cheeses. Stir through until melted.

In a bowl, mix 1 tablespoon of water with the cornflour (cornstarch) to make a smooth paste. Stir the cornflour paste, truffle paste and truffle oil into the cheese mixture, then add some pepper and the nutmeg and remove from the heat. Top with shaved fresh black truffle.

Cook the new potatoes in a saucepan of boiling water until tender. Drain and roughly crush or halve some of the potatoes.

Slice the Beaufort into batons. Cut the remaining Emmental into large triangles and leave the wedge of Bleu d'Auvergne whole.

Slice half of the baguette. Break the cauliflower into florets and dice the apple. Place the cornichons in a ramekin.

ASSEMBLE

Place the warm fondue in the centre of a marble board with the ramekin of cornichons, cauliflower florets and potatoes around it. Place the Beaufort batons to the bottom right of the board, resting on their edges, and place the saucissons near the ramekin of cornichons. Place the baguette slices and remaining baguette pieces to the left and top of the board and fan the prosciutto between them. Place the triangles of Emmental at the top of the board and the Bleu d'Auvergne on the bottom left. Fill the remaining space on the board with the cherries, redcurrants, apple and rosemary and thyme sprigs.

59

Ultimate Game-Day Board

In our house, Sunday is definitely sports day. Whether it's football, cricket or basketball, it is always on in the background while we have a lazy day at home. I don't know a lot about sports, but one thing I do know is that a good snack selection is a must. So, when we have guests over to watch a big match, this epic spread of cheese and nibbles is my go-to.

Dive into this easy, cheesy board, featuring crowd-pleasers creamy Brie and Munster, and snack-food classics like the buffalo wings with a blue cheese dip. A combination of bold flavours and plenty of crunchy, salty bites, this grazing board is guaranteed to please any hungry half-time crowd!

COMPONENTS ···

Cheese
250g (9oz) cream cheese
100g (3½oz) Cheddar, grated, plus
   extra for topping
125g (4½oz) mozzarella ball, cut
   into small pieces
200g (7oz) Cashel Blue cheese
250g (9oz) Old Amsterdam Gouda
200g (7oz) Délice de Bourgogne
100g (3½oz) Petit Munster

Meat
8 shop-bought buffalo wings
50g (1¾oz) sliced salami

Accompaniments
40g (1½oz) sliced dill pickles
200g (7oz) carrots
6 celery sticks
1 cucumber
100g (3½oz) Tenderstem broccoli
handful of orange and red cherry
   tomatoes

For the stuffed mini peppers
oil/butter, for greasing
3 tbsp spring onions (scallions),
   sliced
6 rashers of streaky bacon, cooked
   and sliced

½ tbsp garlic granules
½ tsp chilli powder
½ tsp onion powder
½ tsp cumin
1 tsp Worcestershire sauce
500g (1lb 2 oz) mini mixed
   peppers, halved lengthways,
   seeds and membranes removed
pinch of freshly ground black
   pepper
handful of chives, to garnish

For the blue cheese dip
125ml (4¼oz/generous ½ cup)
   vegetable stock
250ml (8fl oz/1 cup) double (heavy)
   cream, at room temperature
juice of ½ lemon
flaked sea salt and freshly ground
   black pepper
handful of chives, to garnish

Bread and crackers
handful of mini Grissini

Garnish
60g (2oz) rocket (arugula)
bunch of curly-leaf parsley

PREP

Make the stuffed mini peppers

Preheat the oven to 200°C (400°F/Gas Mark 6) and grease a baking tray.

Mix together the cream cheese, spring onions (scallions), bacon, garlic granules, chilli powder, onion powder, cumin, Cheddar, mozzarella, Worcestershire sauce and pepper in a bowl until combined..

Spoon a good amount of cheese filling into each pepper half, then sprinkle over a little more Cheddar, to give it a crispy top. Place on the baking tray cut-side up and bake in the oven for 10–15 minutes until the cheese is melted and golden, then remove and garnish with the chopped chives.

Make the blue cheese dip

Put the stock in a saucepan set over a low heat, then gradually pour in the cream and stir constantly until thick. Gradually crumble in the Cashel blue cheese and stir until you end up with a thick sauce. Remove from the heat. Stir in the lemon juice, season with salt and pepper, then garnish with chives.

Put the blue cheese dip in a heatproof bowl and put the dill pickles in a ramekin.

Heat the shop-bought buffalo wings according to packet instructions and cut the Gouda into bite-sized pieces.

Cut the carrot, celery and cucumber into batons, and break the broccoli into florets. Halve some of the cherry tomatoes.

Remove part of the top of the Délice de Bourgogne by making a cut around the rind on one side, creating an open side for dipping.

ASSEMBLE

On a rectangular tray, with a short side nearest you, place the bowl of blue cheese dip at the bottom and the bowl of dill pickles at the top.

Place the Délice de Bourgogne near the top right and the Munster centre-left of the tray. Fan the carrots, celery, broccoli and cucumber batons around the Délice de Bourgogne. Place the warm buffalo wings at the bottom of the tray on a piece of greaseproof paper to the right of the blue cheese dip, and place the stuffed mini peppers to the left of the dip. Fan folds of salami to the centre-right of the tray and place the Gouda pieces to the left of the salami. Now be creative and fill the gaps in the tray with rocket (arugula), tomatoes, parsley and Grissini.

PAIRINGS

Stuffed mini peppers + rocket (arugula)

Blue cheese dip + buffalo wings

Old Amsterdam Gouda + salami

Délice de Bourgogne + salami + tomato

Petit Munster + dill pickles

Pairs well with a Chardonnay or cold beer

Baked Feta Board

This simple cheeseboard featuring a single star cheese in the form of a baked feta, is perfect for any party. The feta at the centre of the board is quick and simple to make, baked in honey, thyme, almonds and figs. The figs add an extra fruity note to the board and work well with the flavours of the salty cheese and the crunchy, nutty almonds. I serve the cheese with plenty of fresh and crunchy sides which cut through the creaminess of the cheese and make it the ideal summer sharing plate.

COMPONENTS

Cheese
250g (8¾oz) feta

Accompaniments
4 mini cucumbers
200g (7oz) roasted flaked
  almonds
50g (1¾oz) mixed olives

For the baked feta dip
drizzle of olive oil
80ml (2¾fl oz) honey
3 fresh figs, quartered
2 sprigs of thyme
freshly ground black pepper

For the toast crackers
140g (5oz/scant 1 cup) plain
  (all-purpose) flour
¼ tsp bicarbonate of soda
  (baking soda)

40g (1½oz) dried cranberries
100g (3½oz) golden raisins
handful of pumpkin seeds
40g (1½oz) whole flaxseeds
130 g (4½oz) almonds
1 tbsp honey
30g (1oz) soft dark brown sugar
1 tsp flaked sea salt
240ml (8fl oz/1 cup) milk

Bread and crackers
6 Bath Oliver biscuits

Garnish
2 sprigs of thyme

PREP

Make the baked feta dip

Preheat the oven to 200°C (400°F/Gas Mark 6). Place the feta in a small ovenproof dish that you can place on your board. Drizzle the feta with olive oil and bake in the oven for about 6 minutes, until the cheese is springy to the touch but not melted. Remove from the oven and drizzle with honey then return to the oven. Place the figs on a baking tray and bake the cheese and figs for 10 minutes. Remove and season to taste with black pepper, garnish the cheese with thyme sprigs.

Halve the cucumbers lengthways.

Make the toast crackers

Preheat the oven to 180°C (350°F/Gas Mark 4).

Mix together all the ingredients (except the milk) in a bowl. Stir in the milk and mix until the ingredients come together and form a batter. Pour the batter into a 500g (1lb) loaf tin and bake in the oven for 50 minutes until golden brown, risen and an inserted toothpick comes out clean. Remove from the oven, leave to cool, then freeze for 2 hours.

Preheat the oven to 200°C (400°F/Gas Mark 6).

Remove the frozen loaf from the tin and cut it into thin slices, then place the sliced loaf onto a baking tray and bake for about 20 minutes, turning halfway through, until golden. Leave to cool.

ASSEMBLE

Place the dish of warm baked feta in the centre of the cheeseboard. Create a fan of Bath Oliver biscuits along the right side of the feta and arrange the toast crackers at the top and bottom of the board. Arrange the halved cucumbers and figs on the left side of the feta, then fill in the gaps with almonds and olives and garnish with thyme. Dip away!

Pair with a New Zealand Sauvignon Blanc

PAIRINGS

Feta + toast crackers + almonds

Feta + cucumber + thyme

Feta + Bath Oliver biscuits + fresh figs

65

Blue Cheeseboard

If you are not a fan of blue cheese it may be best to skip this page... Okay, now for all the blue cheese lovers, this one is for you. This extravagant and lavish board focuses on dark chocolate, blue cheese, charcuterie and cranberries. A cool blue blend of sweet, spicy, salty, creamy and sharp in this colourful creation featuring our most beloved blue cheeses and sweet and savoury bites. The selection of drinks pairings highlights the amazing variety of flavour profiles on this board.

COMPONENTS

Cheese
30g (1oz) Gorgonzola Dolce
100g (3½oz) Roquefort
100g (3½oz) Stilton
100g (3½oz) Fourme d'Ambert

Meat
150g (5½oz) sliced prosciutto

Accompaniments
100g (3½oz) dark chocolate bar
    (minimum 70% cocoa solids)
50g (1¾oz) floral honey

80g (2¾oz) fig jam
20g (¾oz) raspberries
50g (1¾oz) dried cranberries
20g (¾oz) blueberries
50g (1¾oz) walnuts

Bread and crackers
100g (3½oz) beetroot crackers

Garnish
handful of purple and blue edible flowers

PREP

Cut the Gorgonzola into bite-sized pieces and the Roquefort into triangles. Break the chocolate into chunks. Fill two separate ramekins or bowls with the honey and fig jam.

ASSEMBLE

Place the Stilton on the top-left corner of the board and the Fourme d'Ambert on the middle right section of the board. Place the bowl of fig jam near the Fourme d'Ambert and place the ramekin of honey on the bottom-left of the board, then arrange the triangles of Roquefort near the honey. Place the Gorgonzola at the left-hand bottom of the board and arrange the crackers, prosciutto and chocolate on the board, placing the fruits and nuts in the gaps. Garnish the board with edible flowers.

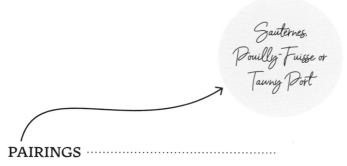

Sauternes, Pouilly-Fuisse or Tawny Port

PAIRINGS

Gorgonzola Dolce + honey + walnuts

Roquefort + honey + raspberries

Stilton + cranberries + edible flowers

Fourme d'Ambert + dark chocolate + blueberries

Easy Crostini

Using crostini to create canapés is easy – they can be topped with anything you want and are a delicious finger food. Crostini translates into 'little crusts' in Italian, and that's what they are: thin, small slices of bread, toasted until crisp and then piled with toppings. They can be made days in advance too, as they keep crisp for ages! Here you'll find four favourite toppings that I consider the perfect flavour pairings.

Gorgeously ripe burrata and fresh, tangy peaches is a classic but underrated flavour combination that you can't go wrong with and it looks very pretty too. Caprese is one of my favourite flavour combinations, whether in the form of the classic salad or as a topping on crunchy pieces of crostini. The combination of ripe, tart blackberries bursting with flavour, soft-style or softened goat's cheese, fresh thyme leaves and crunchy honeycomb makes each bite sing. With the king of cheese, you'll need a good fillet steak to match. Brie, steak and rocket is a dead simple but bold offering with the buttery cheese and rich steak offset by a little fire from the mustard and peppery rocket (arugula). The ideal mix of sweet, salty, fruity and buttery – with a little bit of peppery spice thrown in for good measure. You can serve just one combination or mix and match, depending on how much variety you want.

Makes: 30 crostini

COMPONENTS

For the crostini
artisan-style baguette, cut 5mm (¼-in)-thick
  on the diagonal to make 30 slices
3 tbsp extra virgin olive oil
1 garlic clove, halved
flaked sea salt

PREP

Preheat the oven to 180°C (350°F/Gas Mark 4). Place the bread slices on a baking tray. Brush both sides with the olive oil and sprinkle with salt. Bake on the baking tray for 10–15 minutes until golden, turning them over halfway through and rubbing one side of each slice with the halved garlic.

GRILLED PEACH & BURRATA CROSTINI

Makes: 8 crostini

COMPONENTS

2 ripe peaches, stoned, and each cut into 6 slices
2 x 150g (5½oz) burrata balls
8 crostini
best-quality extra virgin olive oil, for drizzling
freshly ground black pepper

PREP

Place a griddle pan over a medium heat and add the peach slices. Grill until golden, turning halfway through. Spread the burrata cream, scooped from the centre of the two burrata balls, onto the crostini (don't discard the skins: use them to make a salad with fresh tomatoes). Top with 2 or 3 slices of grilled peach and finish with a drizzle of extra virgin olive oil and a sprinkle of black pepper.

PAIRINGS

Grilled peach & burrata crostini + Pinot Grigio

Burrata, tomato & olive oil crostini + crisp, dry rosé

Goat's cheese, blackberry, honeycomb & thyme crostini + white Chablis

Brie de Meaux, steak & rocket crostini + Cabernet Sauvignon

BURRATA, TOMATO & OLIVE OIL CROSTINI

Makes: 10 crostini

COMPONENTS

2 150g (5½oz) burrata balls
10 crostini
400g (14oz) cherry tomatoes, cut into 8
½ bunch of basil, leaves picked
3 tbsp extra virgin olive oil

PREP

Scoop the burrata cream out and spread generously onto the crostini then neatly place sliced tomato onto the bread. Thinly slice the basil and use to garnish the crostini then drizzle with olive oil.

GOAT'S CHEESE, BLACKBERRY, HONEYCOMB & THYME CROSTINI

Makes: 6 crostini

COMPONENTS

160g (5¾oz) soft-style or softened goat's cheese, cut into 5mm-thick slices and left to soften
6 crostini
14–16 blackberries, cut into 3mm (⅛in)-thick slices
120g (4¼oz) piece of honeycomb, cut into teaspoon sized pieces
2 tsp thyme leaves
honey, for drizzling

PREP

Place the goat's cheese on the crostini then top with blackberry slices. Place a piece of honeycomb on each crostini then drizzle with honey and garnish with the thyme leaves.

BRIE DE MEAUX, STEAK & ROCKET CROSTINI

Makes: 8 crostini

COMPONENTS

180g (6¼oz) fillet steak, at room temperature
olive oil, for the steak
1 tsp English mustard
8 crostini
20g (¾oz) baby rocket (arugula)
160g (5¾oz) Brie de Meaux, thinly sliced
flaked sea salt and freshly ground black pepper

PREP

Heat a frying pan (skillet) over a high heat, season the steak with salt and pepper, rub it with oil then add it to the hot pan. Cook for 2 minutes on one side then flip it over and cook for a further 2 minutes (for rare meat – I like it rare but cook it until you are happy). Transfer to a chopping board and leave to rest for 10 minutes before slicing it as thinly as you can.

Spread a thin layer of mustard on your crostini, neatly add the rocket (arugula) leaves, then place a slice of Brie on top. Finish with the gorgeous steak, adding a little salt and pepper to season.

71

The G.O.A.T. (the greatest of all time)

This is the pinnacle of cheeseboards. Not for the faint of heart, this five-cheese masterpiece showcases world-renowned, award-winning cheese in one beautiful board. The cheese is the hero here, so the accompaniments have been kept simple, but they are all perfectly matched to help showcase the best of these already-brilliant cheeses. As with any award winner, these cheeses deserve something a little special to be served alongside, and an aged Burgundy Chardonnay really fits the bill with these flavours. This stunning board is guaranteed to make mouths water at your next gathering.

COMPONENTS

Cheese
200g (7oz) Pecorino Moliterno al Tartufo, Italy, 2017 winner
250g (9oz) Manchego DO Gran Reserva, Dehesa de los Llanos, Spain, 2012 winner
250g (9oz) Rogue River Blue, Rogue Creamery of Central Point, Oregon USA, 2019 winner
250g (9oz) Le Gruyère AOP, Cremo von Mühlenen, Switzerland, 2015 winner
250g (9oz) Brie de Meaux, Rénard Gillard, France, 2007 winner

Meat
100g (3½oz) sliced wild boar salami
70g (2½oz) sliced prosciutto

Accompaniments
¼ cucumber
6 strawberries
50g (1¾oz) raspberry jam
handful of raspberries
handful of blueberries
50g (1¾oz) almonds
40g (1½oz) shelled pistachios
handful of large green olives

Bread and crackers
125g (4½oz) buttermilk wafers

Garnish
20g (¾oz) thyme sprigs
20g (¾oz) rosemary sprigs

PREP

Cut the Pecorino and Manchego into long triangles. Break some of the Rogue River Blue into chunks, leaving 5–7.5cm (2–3in) of cheese on the rind. Cut some of the Gruyère into batons and leave the rest intact, with a few chunks broken off.

Cut the salami into thin 'coins' and cut the cucumber into small half-moons. Halve the strawberries lengthways.

Put the raspberry jam in a small bowl or ramekin.

ASSEMBLE

Place the whole wedge of Brie in the middle of the board with the bowl or ramekin of jam next to it. Shingle the Pecorino triangles and Manchego triangles to the left of the board, then pile the chunks of Rogue River Blue along with the remaining whole cheese on the right side of the board. Place the Gruyère batons and remaining whole cheese on the board near the Rogue River Blue. Place the salami 'coins' – loosely folded – on the board between the Pecorino and Manchego triangles. Lay the prosciutto next to the Gruyère batons. Fill the gaps with fruits, nuts, olives, cucumber and wafers. Garnish with the thyme and rosemary.

Pair with an aged Burgundy Chardonnay

PAIRINGS

Pecorino + almonds + wild boar salami

Manchego + raspberry jam + fresh raspberries

Rogue River Blue + raspberry jam

Gruyère + blueberries + wild boar salami

Brie + strawberries + thyme

75

THROUGHOUT THE YEAR BOARDS

Valentine's Day Fondue for Two

The ultimate cheese-lover's board – and what is more romantic than a fondue centrepiece for two? This features the most romantic cheese ever made, Coeur de Neufchâtel. The heart shape is said to have originated during the Hundred Years' War when English soldiers were stationed in Normandy. The French farm girls, all of whom made cheese, fell in love with them and started making heart-shaped cheeses. Of course, you can dip a whole range of delicacies into a fondue, but I do love to add something a little bit different, some may say even more naughty than a French dipping cheese...maple-glazed bacon. This is a must-try: the bacon highlights the sweetness of the cheese and creates a taste sensation of salty, creamy, crunchy perfection.

COMPONENTS

Cheese
200g (7oz) Emmental
200g (7oz) Gruyère
100g (3½oz) Comté
1 Coeur de Neufchâtel

Meat
8 rashers of maple-glazed
   streaky bacon
40g (1½oz) sliced smoked
   sausage
80g (2¾oz) sliced prosciutto
   di Parma

Accompaniments
1 red apple
50g (1¾oz) strawberry jam
bunch of redcurrants
large bunch of red grapes
50g (1¾oz) cherries
50g (1¾oz) strawberries
50g (1¾oz) raspberries
6 milk chocolate hearts

For the fondue
1 garlic clove
200ml (7fl oz/scant 1 cup) dry
   white wine
1 tsp lemon juice
1 tsp cornflour (cornstarch)

Bread and crackers
½ crusty baguette

Garnish
Small handful edible flowers
4 rosemary sprigs

PREP

Make the fondue

Grate the Emmental and Gruyère and cut the garlic clove in half. Rub the inside of a fondue pan with the garlic. Add the wine and lemon juice to the pan over a medium heat until boiling. Reduce the heat and gradually stir in the grated cheeses until melted, stirring all the time. Put the cornflour (cornstarch) in a small bowl, add 1 tablespoon of water and whisk until smooth, making sure there are no lumps.

Add the cornflour to the cheese mixture and cook gently until the mixture is smooth – don't let it boil or it will burn. Remove from the heat.

Cut the Comté into triangles. Fry the bacon in a frying pan (skillet) over a medium heat until crispy. Drain on kitchen paper (paper towels). Slice the baguette and thinly slice the apple. Put the jam in a ramekin or small bowl.

ASSEMBLE

Place the warm fondue pan at the top right of the board, and position the Coeur de Neufchâtel to the middle-left. Arrange the baguette slices and crispy bacon around the fondue pan and place the ramekin or bowl of strawberry jam in the lower right corner. Surround the Coeur de Neufchâtel with the

smoked sausage slices, prosciutto di Parma and redcurrants. Fan the Comté triangles at opposite sides of the board. Fill the gaps with the grapes, sliced apple and remaining fruit and chocolate hearts. Garnish with edible flowers and rosemary.

Pairs with Riesling

PAIRINGS

Fondue + maple-glazed streaky bacon

Fondue + apple + smoked sausage

Comté + cherries + rosemary

Coeur de Neufchâtel + strawberry jam + strawberries

St Patrick's Day Board

Grab your Guinness and celebrate the most Irish of holidays with this St Paddy's Day cheeseboard. Being part-Irish I may be biased, but I think Ireland is home to some of the most amazing cheeses, due to the luscious pastures that the animals graze on. What better time to celebrate these wonderful cheeses than on St Paddy's Day. It would be remiss of me not to suggest pairing the cheeses with a Guinness, but for a lighter tipple, an oaked Chardonnay is a lovely match with the Durrus.

COMPONENTS

Cheese
150g (5½oz) Coolea cheese
200g (7oz) Gubbeen farmhouse
200g (7oz) Cashel Blue
150g (5½oz) Durrus farmhouse
100g (3½oz) Cahill's garlic and
    herb Cheddar

Accompaniments
handful of orange tomatoes
¼ cucumber
10g (⅓oz) white radishes
1 green apple
2 celery sticks
5 cauliflower florets
80g (2¾oz) Negroni Chutney
    (page 162)
handful of dried apricots
30g (1oz) blanched almonds
5 spears of jarred white
    asparagus
10g (⅓oz) silverskin pickled
    onions
bunch of green grapes
10g (⅓oz) green olives
20g (¾oz) mini gherkins

Bread and crackers
30g (1oz) white buttermilk
    crackers

Garnish
5 dried orange slices
20g (¾oz) flat-leaf parsley
3 orange pansies
20g (¾oz) rosemary sprigs
2 thyme sprigs

PREP

Cut the Coolea cheese and the Gubbeen farmhouse into batons and crumble the Cashel Blue. Crumble the Durrus farmhouse and cut the top off the Cahill's Cheddar.

Slice most of the tomatoes, keeping a couple of smaller tomatoes whole, thinly slice the cucumber and radishes, then cut the apple (skin on) into thin wedges. Cut the celery into batons and break the cauliflower florets into smaller pieces. Put the chutney into a ramekin or small bowl.

ASSEMBLE

Place the Negroni chutney at the bottom right of the board. Place the Coolea and Gubbeen farmhouse batons on the right, with the other orange ingredients: the tomatoes, dried orange slices and apricots. Along the middle of the board arrange the crumbled Cashel Blue and Durrus farmhouse with the other pale ingredients: the radish, almonds, some of the apple, white asparagus, silverskin onions cauliflower florets and buttermilk crackers. Place the Cahill's Cheddar cheese on the left of the board with the other green ingredients: the celery, grapes, parsley, more apple, cucumber slices (arranged as a rose), olives and gherkins. The desired effect here is to have a subtle Irish flag (green, white and orange). Garnish the board with the pansies, rosemary and thyme.

PAIRINGS

Coolea cheese + dried apricots

Gubbeen farmhouse cheese + white asparagus + tomato

Cashel Blue + apple

Durrus farmhouse cheese + Negroni chutney

Pairs with Guinness or oaked Chardonnay

Easter Board

Easter offers a great opportunity to entertain. Part of the beauty of this board is that it is a great addition to your Easter spread and it looks impressive, but doesn't require any cooking. Full of spring beauties, it features seasonal cheese specials and a few chocolate eggs thrown in for good measure. I like to add a bit of cold lamb leftover from the Easter dinner to make the board extra delicious. Spring seasonal cheeses such as Gouda and Basque sheep's cheese are beautifully tasty due to the lucious pastures that the cow or goats feed on in the spring months which makes the cheeses taste rich and complex.

COMPONENTS

Cheese
200g (7oz) Basque sheep's
   cheese
200g (7oz) Gouda
150g (5½oz) Parmigiano-
   Reggiano
125g (4½oz) mini Camembert
1 Ragstone goat's cheese log

Meat
½ joint of cold roast lamb
80g (2¾oz) sliced prosciutto

Accompaniments
handful of thin asparagus spears
100g (3½oz) tenderstem broccoli
3 baby carrots with tops
9 strawberries
¼ cucumber
120g (4¼oz) piece of honeycomb

30g (1oz) mint sauce
300g (10½oz) chocolate eggs
   (I use a mixture of mini
   sugar-coated eggs and larger
   chocolate eggs)
20g (¾oz) cornichons
small handful of shelled
   pistachios
20g (¾oz) almonds
handful of dried apricots
8 leftover roast potatoes

Bread and crackers
handful of fennel seed tarallini
6 malted milk biscuits

Garnish
handful of thyme sprigs
bunch of curly-leaf parsley

PREP

Steam the asparagus and tenderstem broccoli for 5 minutes and leave to cool. Cut the Basque sheep's cheese and Gouda into triangles. Keep the Camembert whole and cut a few slices from the goat's cheese. Cut the Parmigiano-Reggiano into batons. Peel the carrots, leaving the tops in place, and halve them lengthways.

Slice the cold roast lamb.

Halve most of the strawberries. Thinly slice the cucumber. Place the honeycomb in a ramekin or bowl and the mint sauce in a separate bowl or jar. Place the mini sugar coated chocolate eggs in a ramekin or bowl.

ASSEMBLE

Place the whole Camembert at the bottom right of the board with the carrots, asparagus and tenderstem broccoli nearby and fan the triangles of Basque sheep's cheese and Gouda near the top right of the board. Place the goat's cheese (whole cheese and slices) in the top left corner of the board. Place the honeycomb near the fanned-out cheese triangles, along with the fennel seed tarallini. Shingle the Parmigiano-Reggiano along the bottom left corner of the

board. Fold the prosciutto slices near the goat's cheese and place the cornichons nearby. Put the ramekin or bowl of mini sugar coated chocolate eggs on the left of the board and fan the malted milk biscuits around it. Fill the gaps with the strawberries, cucumber, remaining chocolate eggs, pistachios, almonds and dried apricots. Garnish with the thyme and parsley. Serve the lamb, mint sauce and potatoes separately.

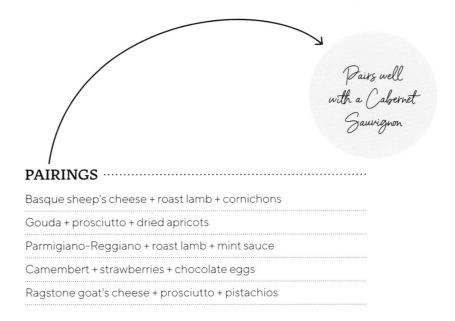

Pairs well with a Cabernet Sauvignon

PAIRINGS

Basque sheep's cheese + roast lamb + cornichons

Gouda + prosciutto + dried apricots

Parmigiano-Reggiano + roast lamb + mint sauce

Camembert + strawberries + chocolate eggs

Ragstone goat's cheese + prosciutto + pistachios

Summer Solstice Board

Board Style: Ceramic platter
Serves: 2

Ever since I was a little girl, my parents have had a summer solstice party and I've always loved the idea of celebrating the start of summer. When you live in rainy London, trust me, a bit of sunshine is worthy of a celebration. I serve this go-to summer board at the solstice party every year and it has never failed me. It is beautifully bright and bursting with seasonal cheese and refreshing produce.

COMPONENTS

Cheese
300g (10½oz) Parmigiano-
 Reggiano
200g (7oz) Gouda
8 mozzarella bocconcini
120g (4¼oz) Ragstone goat's
 cheese log
125g (4½oz) mini Camembert

Meat
20g (¾oz) sliced prosciutto
40g (1½oz) saucisson

Accompaniments
80g (2¾oz) watermelon
¼ Cantaloupe melon
1 orange

1 peach
¼ cucumber
30g (1oz) fig jam, plus extra
 to serve
bunch of red grapes
small handful of walnuts

Bread and crackers
4 breadsticks

Garnish
3 rosemary sprigs
handful of edible flowers

PREP

Crumble off about half the Parmigiano-Reggiano, leaving about 5cm (2in) left at the end. Cut the Gouda into evenly-sized, neat triangles. Place the mozzarella bocconcini into a ramekin. Halve the goat's cheese log. Slice the saucission into 5mm (¼in)-thick pieces. Cut the watermelon into small triangles, the Cantaloupe melon into thin wedges and the orange into 5mm (¼in)-thick slices. Halve the peach, remove the stone and cut one half into wedges. Thinly slice the cucumber.

Put the fig jam in a ramekin or bowl.

ASSEMBLE

Place the two ramekins of mozzarella bocconcini and fig jam on the board just off centre. Place the Parmigiano-Reggiano (whole and crumbled pieces) to the top right and the goat's cheese (both halves) and Camembert together near the centre of the board. Fan the Gouda slices on the bottom right and bottom left of the board. Place the grapes and peach near the Parmigiano-Reggiano, along with the breadsticks, and fan the cucumber and watermelon slices near the ramekin of mozzarella bocconcini. Place the melon wedges and orange slices at the bottom of the board, near the Gouda triangles, and fan the prosciutto near the peach. Fill the gaps with the walnuts and slices of saucisson and garnish with the rosemary sprigs and flowers.

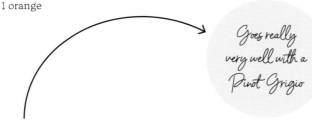

Goes really very well with a Pinot Grigio

PAIRINGS

Parmigiano-Reggiano + walnuts + grapes

Gouda + prosciutto + Cantaloupe melon

Mozzarella bocconcini + peaches + walnuts

Camembert + fig jam + rosemary

Goat's cheese + walnuts + fig jam

The Cookout Board

Whether you are cozying up to a fireplace or sitting around a fire on a camping holiday, this spread is the ultimate autumn evening cheeseboard. With rich meats, strong smoky cheeses and sweet gooey s'mores, it's ideal for sharing near the fireside. A cool, refreshing Paloma cocktail is the perfect accompaniment as the sour-sharp flavours cut through the sweet flavours of the board.

COMPONENTS

Cheese
100g (3½oz) smoked Cheddar
1 Petit Munster
150g (5½oz) Jarlsberg
200g (7oz) Stilton
100g (3½oz) Parmigiano-
    Reggiano

Meat
20 cocktail sausages
80g (2¾oz) sliced bresaola

Accompaniments
50g (1¾oz) candy-striped
    beetroot (beets)
1 apple
½ Galia melon
30g (1oz) cranberry sauce
    or chutney
1 toffee apple
2 bunches of red grapes
handful of blackberries
handful of blueberries
50g (1¾oz) pecans
handful of almonds

For the hot honey cocktail sausages
1 tsp vegetable oil, for frying
3 tbsp Hot Honey (page 165)
1 tbsp orange juice
½ tsp ground cinnamon
flaked sea salt

For the s'mores
20 jumbo marshmallows
20 chocolate digestive biscuits

Bread and crackers
5 water biscuits

Garnish
8 mini sparklers

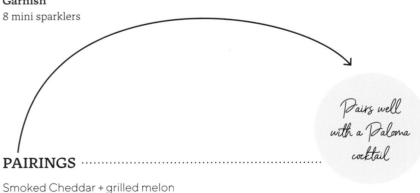

Pairs well with a Paloma cocktail

PAIRINGS

Smoked Cheddar + grilled melon

Petit Munster + hot honey sausages

Jarlsberg + blackberries

Stilton + pecans + chocolate digestive biscuits

Parmigiano-Reggiano + bresaola

PREP

Make the hot honey cocktail sausages
To make the hot honey cocktail sausages, heat a large frying pan (skillet) over a medium heat, pour in the oil and then once warm, add the cocktail sausages and fry for 10 minutes until browned all over. Mix the hot honey, orange juice, cinnamon and a pinch of salt in a small bowl, then pour the mixture over the sausages and cook for a minute or two until the mixture becomes sticky and clings to the sausages. Pop a skewer through the sausages and leave to cool down before placing them on the board. Slice the beetroot thinly and cut the apple into thin wedges (skin on).

Make the s'mores
Place the digestives on a plate, chocolate side up. Thread two of the marshmallows onto a skewer and toast over an open flame. Place the marshmallows on top of one of the digestives and then top with another digestive, chocolate side down. Repeat until you have used all of the digestives and marshmallows.

Cut the melon into thin wedges. Heat a griddle pan over a medium-high heat, add the slices of melon and grill for 3–4 minutes, until the flesh has griddle marks. Turn them over and cook for a further 3–4 minutes. Remove from the griddle pan and set aside.
Cut the smoked Cheddar into cubes and half of the Jarlsberg and all of the Parmigiano-Reggiano into triangles. Cut the remaining Jarlsberg into batons. Put the cranberry sauce or chutney in a small bowl or ramekin.

ASSEMBLE

Arrange the cheeses on a square board, placing them equidistant from another and fanning out the triangles of Jarlsberg and Parmigiano-Reggiano and stacking the batons of Jarlsberg. Place the bowl of honey sausages on the board with toothpicks for piercing and fan the bresaola down the middle of the board. Put the bowl or ramekin of cranberry sauce or chutney on the board to the centre-right. Place the water biscuits on the top right corner of the board along with the toffee apple, then lay the apple and beetroot (beet) slices on the bottom right corner and the grilled melon wedges fanned out on the left-hand side. Place a bunch of grapes either side of the board and fill in the gaps with the fresh berries and nuts. Top with sparklers.

PALOMA COCKTAIL

COMPONENTS

Serves 1

juice of half a pink grapefruit
1½ shots of good tequila
½ shot of agave syrup or sugar syrup
about 75ml soda water
a squirt of fresh lime juice (optional)
flaked sea salt (optional)

METHOD

Mix the grapefruit juice, tequila and sugar syrup until well mixed.
Pour over a glass with ice and top up with soda water. You could add a squirt of lime juice, which is nice, and you could also rim the glass with salt.

93

Halloween Cheeseboard

Leave the sweets to the kids on Halloween night and enjoy this delicious cheeseboard instead. This party platter is the ultimate holiday centrepiece, full of cheesy treats, spooky crackers, scarily stinky cheese and autumnal ingredients. Impress your guests with this macabre crowd-pleasing, bumper selection of five cheeses, featuring sweet and savoury favourites like Cabrales Blue and Manchego. A Spanish Tempranillo is just what you need to warm up the taste buds as autumn sets in, and is the perfect pairing with these seasonal cheeses.

COMPONENTS

Cheese
150g (5½oz) mature Manchego
100g (3½oz) Sparkenhoe Red Leicester
150g (5½oz) mini Brie
100g (3½oz) Shropshire Blue
200g (7oz) Cabrales Blue

Meat
200g (7oz) sliced spicy salami

Accompaniments
60g (2oz) cornichons
120g (4¼oz) piece of honeycomb
2 large bunches of black grapes
1 large fresh fig
2 handfuls of walnuts
handful of pecans

Bread and crackers
1 quantity of Toast Crackers (page 64)
7 or 8 puff-pastry cheese twists

Garnish
variety of mini pumpkins
5 dried orange slices
20g (¾oz) rosemary sprigs

PREP

Cut the Manchego into thin triangles, cut the Sparkenhoe Red Leicester into 1cm (½in) cubes, and cut the mini Brie and Shropshire Blue into wedges.
    Place the cornichons in a small ramekin or bowl.

ASSEMBLE

Place the pumpkins at various intervals on and around the slate and the board. Place the mini Brie near the centre of the board with the ramekin of cornichons and shingle the Manchego triangles along the middle of the board. Create two piles of cubed Red Leicester on the board, put the Cabrales Blue on the left of the board and the Shropshire Blue on the right, opposite the Cabrales. Place the honeycomb on top of the Brie. Fill in all the gaps with the grapes, fig, salami, nuts, dried orange slices, toast crackers and cheese twists, garnishing the board with sprigs of rosemary to finish.

Goes very nicely with a Tempranillo

PAIRINGS

Manchego + spicy salami + fresh figs

Sparkenhoe Red Leicester + spicy salami

Brie + honeycomb

Shropshire Blue + grapes + cheese toast

Cabrales Blue + fresh figs

Holiday Gather Board

Before you enter the madness of the Christmas entertaining season, celebrate the best of late autumn offerings – if this board doesn't get you into the holiday spirit, we don't know what will! When you have a Champagne-doused cheese, you know you're onto something a little bit special. This expertly curated spread includes some of our favourite seasonal items and a whole lot of original flavours. Created with hosting and entertaining in mind, it's packed with our most luxurious and crowd-pleasing cheeses and accompaniments.

COMPONENTS

Cheese
250g (9oz) Mimolette
200g (7oz) Sparkenhoe Red Leicester
200g (7oz) Comté
150g (5½oz) Selles-sur-Cher
250g (9oz) Camembert
150g (5½oz) mini Brie
200g (7oz) Shropshire Blue
180g (6¼oz) Langres

Meat
200g (7oz) sliced salami
200g (7oz) sliced prosciutto
150g (5½oz) sliced bresaola

Accompaniments
100g (3½oz) marinated artichoke hearts
150g (5½oz) cornichons
50g (1¾oz) mixed olives
1 pomegranate
1 pear
5 fresh apricots
10 fresh figs
100g (3½oz) fig and almond cake
2 stems of redcurrants
handful of Marcona almonds
3 persimmons
120g (4¼oz) piece of honeycomb

Bread and crackers
1 French baguette
20 Toast Crackers (page 64)
handful of star butter crackers

Garnish
5 rosemary sprigs
4 dried orange slices
3 sage sprigs
baubles and Christmas decorations of your choice

PREP

Cut the Mimolette into small triangles and crumble a tiny bit of Red Leicester off the end (leaving the rest of the cheese intact). Cut the Comté into long triangles. Cut some Selles-sur-Cher into chunks and some into smaller slices.

Place the artichoke hearts, cornichons and olives in three separate bowls or ramekins.

Cut the pomegranate in half and remove a few of the seeds from each, keep the halves intact. Slice the pears. Halve or slice most of the apricots and figs.

Slice half of the baguette and slice the fig and almond cake.

ASSEMBLE

Place the Camembert just off-centre on the board and top it with the mini Brie, a few redcurrants and a small sprig of rosemary. Place the Selles-sur-Cher nearby, then space the remaining cheeses around the board. Add the bowl or ramekin of artichoke hearts to the top of the board, the cornichons and olives on the right of the board, and the baguette to the left. Fan the salami slices along the centre of the board, arranging the Marcona almonds and sliced figs in rows alongside. Shingle a pile of the toast crackers along the top of the board and a second pile along the bottom. Place the prosciutto near the bread, and the bresaola near the bottom of the board. Fill in the gaps with fanned-out pear slices, pomegranate halves, fig and almond cake, dried orange slices, apricots, persimmons, honeycomb, star butter crackers and remaining figs and redcurrants. Garnish with rosemary and sage.

Pair everything with a glass of Champagne

PAIRINGS

Mimolette + pear

Sparkenhoe Red Leicester + cornichons

Comté + fresh apricots + bresaola

Selles-sur-Cher + fig and almond cake

Camembert + fresh figs + honeycomb

Brie + pear + cornichons

Shropshire Blue + fresh figs + honeycomb

Langres + Marcona almonds

A Festive Cheese Wreath

Christmas boards have come a long way from a basic plate of cheese, thrown together in a panic. One of my favourite creations is the cheese wreath: cheeses, meats and festive accompaniments arranged to look like a Christmas wreath. This board – a form of edible art – is the perfect Christmas party centrepiece: your holiday decor just got much tastier! Enjoy the cheeses with a Christmas martini: the tart, fruity cocktail is a match made in heaven with the Brie and Camembert.

COMPONENTS

Cheese
2 x 55g (2oz) Crottin de Chavignol
150g (5½oz) mini Brie
125g (4½oz) mini Camembert

Meat
50g (1¾oz) sliced salami
70g (2½oz) sliced prosciutto di Parma

Accompaniments
100g (3½oz) piece of honeycomb
bunch of red grapes
50g (1¾oz) pecans
runny honey, for drizzling

Bread and crackers
8 Toast Crackers (page 64)
20g (¾oz) star cheese crackers

Garnish
2 large bunches of rosemary
2 large bunches of fresh bay leaves

Pairs well with the Christmas martini

PAIRINGS

Crottin de Chavignol + honeycomb

Brie + pecans + grapes + salami

Camembert + salami + honeycomb

PREP

Halve the Crottin de Chavignol. Slice the Brie into triangles. Place the honeycomb into a small bowl or ramekin with a honey drizzler.

Create a salami 'rose'. Take a piece of the salami and fold it over the rim of the glass. Repeat with more slices, overlapping them as you go, until you've covered the whole rim. Keep adding pieces – the more salami you use, the fuller the rose will be. Hold the meat in place and rotate the glass so that it's upside down on the board and the rose is facing upwards. Remove the glass carefully and your rose is ready to position on the board.

ASSEMBLE

Start with a greenery base, arranging a flat layer of rosemary and bay leaves in a ring all the way around the board, with the needles facing both inwards and outwards. Add the ramekin or bowl of honeycomb in a gap in the rosemary ring and place the salami 'rose' and Camembert opposite it on the other side of the board. Divide the prosciutto di Parma into two piles on either side of the board. Add the Crottin de Chavignol and Brie triangles on top of the leaves, keeping space between each cheese and leaving room for the other items. Place the grapes, pecans and crackers around the ring, filling in the gaps. Finally, drizzle honey over the Camembert and place a sprig of rosemary on top.

CHRISTMAS SPRITZ

COMPONENTS

Serves 1

For the rosemary simple syrup
250ml/9fl oz/1 cup water
200g/7oz/1 cup granulated sugar
8 rosemary sprigs

125ml/4¼ fl oz cranberry juice
1 tbsp orange juice
1 shot of non-alcoholic gin (optional)
about 75ml soda water
ice cubes

Garnish
1 orange zest twist
3 fresh cranberries

METHOD

Make the rosemary simple syrup
In a small pan, stir together the water and the sugar. Place over a medium heat, bring to the boil and reduce to a simmer. Add the rosemary sprigs and simmer for 2–3 minutes, until all the sugar is completely dissolved. Remove from the heat and leave to fully cool. Strain the syrup into a sterilized bottle and store in the fridge for up to 1 month.

Pour the cranberry juice, orange juice and 1 shot of the rosemary simple syrup into a tall glass and stir well. Add the alcohol-free gin, if using, and stir again. Fill the glass two thirds full of ice and then top with the soda water. Gently stir to combine, one final time. Garnish with the orange zest twist and the cranberries.

CHRISTMAS MARTINI

COMPONENTS

Serves 2

4 tbsp vodka
4 tbsp 100% cranberry juice
2 tbsp Cointreau
2 tbsp lemon juice
4 tsp maple syrup

Garnish
4 rosemary sprigs
4 fresh cranberries

METHOD

Put the vodka, cranberry juice, Cointreau, lemon juice and maple syrup into a cocktail shaker, then add a few ice cubes. Cover and shake for 15 seconds until chilled. Divide between two martini glasses and garnish each cocktail with rosemary sprigs and a couple of cranberries.

103

Boxing Day Party Board

UNPOPULAR OPINION ALERT: although I love Christmas Day, I prefer a Boxing Day walk with my family and a lazy day on the sofa grazing on a good cheeseboard. Put all those tasty Christmas Day leftover cheeses to good use and try this board with turkey, roast potatoes and a whole lot of crowd-pleasing cheese. A particularly harmonious pairing is a glass of Merlot with the Vacherin Mont d'Or, as the rich creaminess of the cheese balances out the dry fruitiness of the wine. Use whatever you have left in the fridge, get creative and add it to the board!

COMPONENTS

Cheese
400g (14oz) Vacherin Mont d'Or
250g (9oz) Colston Bassett
  Stilton
100g (3½oz) Beaufort
200g (7oz) Délice de Bourgogne

Meat
400g (14oz) sliced leftover turkey
300g (10½oz) sliced leftover ham

Accompaniments
80g (2¾oz) cranberry sauce
50g (1¾oz) pickled walnuts
15 leftover roast potatoes
3 clementines
1 soft-leaf lettuce

Bread and crackers
5 soft bread rolls
100g (3½oz) sourdough crackers
5 water biscuits

Garnish
bunch of chives, sniped to 5cm
  (2in) lengths
2 rosemary sprigs
4 mint sprigs

PREP

Slice off half of the Vacherin Mont d'Or lid to prepare it for spooning out. Place the cranberry sauce and pickled walnuts in two separate ramekins or bowls and the leftover potatoes into a larger bowl. Cut the Délice de Bourgogne cheese into small wedges. Peel and segment two of the clementines.

ASSEMBLE

First things first, with a short side of the board facing you, place the Vacherin on the top-left, with a spoon. Place the Stilton to the right and crumble off a little onto the board. Arrange the Beaufort piece at the middle-left of the board and the wedges of Délice de Bourgogne below it. Put the bowl of potatoes in the bottom right corner and the smaller bowls or ramekins of cranberry sauce and pickled walnuts near the middle of the board. Place a bed of lettuce and the soft rolls at the bottom of the board near potatoes and the clementines on the top right. Arrange the turkey and ham slices in rows along the board, the turkey near the rolls and the ham near the Vacherin and Stilton, and place rows of crackers near the Vacherin. Place the biscuits below the ham. Garnish with the herbs.

PAIRINGS

Pair with white Burgundy or Merlot

Vacherin Mont d'Or + roast potatoes

Colston Bassett Stilton + pickled walnuts

Beaufort + cranberry sauce

Délice de Bourgogne + clementines

New Year's Eve Ultimate Celebration Board

This is an epic, indulgent cheeseboard which will get the guests talking for all the right reasons this New Year's Eve. For ultimate opulence and celebration, I've selected some crowd-pleasing favourites with a touch of glitz that are ideal for sharing: stunning Délice de Bourgogne, Parmigiano-Reggiano and Ossau-Iraty. Paired with rich dark chocolate, and fresh 24-carat-gold-coated strawberries, this seriously stunning cheeseboard is guaranteed to wow.

COMPONENTS

Cheese
250g (9oz) Ossau-Iraty
200g (7oz) mature Cheddar
250g (9oz) Parmigiano-Reggiano
1 small (100g/3½oz) Délice de Bourgogne
150g (5½oz) Selles-sur-Cher
180g (6¼oz) Langres

Accompaniments
150g (5oz) quince paste
100g (3½oz) dark chocolate (70% cocoa solids)
8 strawberries

handful of cherries
3 fresh figs
stem of redcurrants
120g (4¼oz) piece of honeycomb
handful of Marcona almonds

Garnish
8 sheets edible gold leaf
4 mini indoor sparklers

Champagne - of course

PAIRINGS

Ossau-Iraty + dark chocolate + fresh figs

Mature Cheddar + quince + redcurrants

Parmigiano-Reggiano + fresh figs

Délice de Bourgogne + dark chocolate + fresh figs

Selles-sur-cher + honeycomb + fresh figs

Langres + Champagne + fresh figs

PREP

Slice the Ossau-Iraty into triangles. Cut the Cheddar and quince paste into 5cm (2in)-thick slices then gently, using a small star-shaped cookie cutter, cut stars from the Cheddar and quince paste. Break the chocolate into bite-sized pieces. Break some small chunks off the Parmigiano-Reggiano. Decorate the strawberries and half of the cherries with edible gold leaf by gently wrapping a small sheet around each fruit. Quarter the figs. Cut a triangle from the Délice de Bourgogne.

ASSEMBLE

Place the two whole cheeses and the Délice de Bourgogne at the centre-right of the large round board or platter and fan pieces of the Ossau-Iraty on the left and right. Arrange the quartered figs down the centre and the cherries and redcurrants near the Délice de Bourgogne and Selles-sur-Cher. Place the chocolate pieces near the Langres and fan the Cheddar and quince-paste stars up the board or platter from the bottom. Place the large piece of Parmigiano-Reggiano and the chunks at the bottom of the board or platter. Place the honeycomb near the Délice de Bourgogne and Selles-sur-Cher and fill in the gaps on the board with Marcona almonds. Gently lay the strawberries on the board. When serving, light the mini indoor sparklers and then add them to the board.

AROUND
THE WORLD
BOARDS

Great British Cheeseboard

Board Style: Wooden chopping board
Serves: 3–5

From brilliant blue to melting Baron Bigod Brie, here are the best cheeses that British cheesemakers have to offer. Britain has a proud history of cheesemaking that stretches back millennia, with our cool, wet climate and lush pastures helping to create one of the world's richest dairy traditions. What would the world be without Cheddar and pickle? If you can't get your hands on a Lincolnshire plum bread, a fruity tea loaf would be a nice substitute: it's those fruity, sticky hits of raisins in a lightly spiced loaf that you're looking for – it works so well with these cheeses.

COMPONENTS

Cheese
200g (7oz) Westcombe Cheddar
200g (7oz) Appleby's Cheshire
130g (4½oz) Dorstone goat's cheese
200g (7oz) Cropwell Bishop Stilton
250g (9oz) Baron Bigod

Meat
8 slices of British farmhouse thick-sliced ham

Accompaniments
1 red apple (I like Gala)
4 radishes

150g (5½oz) My Tomato Chutney (page 160)
3 celery sticks (with leaves intact)
4 large gherkins
200g (7oz) vine cherry tomatoes
10 silverskin onions
handful of watercress

Bread and crackers
1 Lincolnshire plum bread
8 Digestive biscuits

PREP

Cut the Westcombe Cheddar into long triangles, cut the Appleby Cheshire into cubes, and cut the Dorstone in half on the diagonal.

Slice the apple (skin on), slice the plum bread, thinly slice or quarter the radishes and put the tomato chutney in a ramekin. Cut the celery into batons, keeping the leaves intact. Halve the gherkins lengthways and halve some of the tomatoes and silverskin onions.

ASSEMBLE

Place the ramekin of tomato chutney in the centre of the board. Fan folded slices of ham on the top left of the board and place the Stilton, Cheddar triangles and Baron Bigod down the right side of the board. Put the bread slices next to the Stilton. Place the cubed Cheshire on the left of the board and the Dorstone goat's cheese at the bottom of the board. Arrange the biscuits near the goat's cheese. Fill the gaps with sliced apple, celery batons, gherkins, silverskin onions, watercress, sliced radishes and tomatoes.

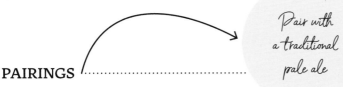

Pair with a traditional pale ale

PAIRINGS

Westcombe Cheddar + gherkins + ham

Appleby's Cheshire + apple + tomato chutney

Dorstone goat's cheese + tomatoes

Cropwell Bishop Stilton + celery

Baron Bigod + watercress + apple

Champs-Élysées Board

A full French feast where cheese is the star of the show, and the accompaniments are simple but effective. Saucissons and French-inspired nibbles all elevate the rich flavours of the artisan cheeses. You'll appreciate the simplicity after just one bite of the Brie de Meaux Dongé that is beautifully buttery paired with a cherry compote. The compote's sweetness with a slight sharpness works so well with this creamy soft cheese, creating the perfect texture and flavour pairing. Try pairing the board with fruity reds like Beaujolais or a refined red Burgundy.

PREP

Slice half of the Sainte-Maure de Touraine into discs, cut the Comté into triangles and slice the Morbier widthways.

Cut half of the saucisson into 'coins'. Fill a ramekin or bowl with cherry compote.

ASSEMBLE

Place your cheeses around the edge of the plate, working clockwise with the Fourme d'Ambert at the top and leaving plenty of room between each one. Fill in the gaps with the ramekin of compote, saucisson 'coins' and whole mini saucisson, blueberries, blackberries, red grapes and almonds.

Serve with the baguette.

COMPONENTS

Cheese
100g (3½oz) Sainte-Maure de
  Touraine
150g (5½oz) Comté
50g (1¾oz) Morbier
80g (2¾oz) Fourme d'Ambert
200g (7oz) Brie de Meaux Dongé
70g (2½oz) Reblochon

Meat
100g (3½oz) mini saucisson

Accompaniments
30g (1oz) cherry compote
handful of blueberries
handful of blackberries
bunch of red grapes
10g (¼oz) almonds

Bread and crackers
1 French baguette

PAIRINGS

Sainte-Maure de Touraine + blackberries

Comté + cherry compote

Morbier + saucisson

Fourme d'Ambert + grapes

Brie de Meaux Dongé + cherry compote

Reblochon + cherry compote + blueberries

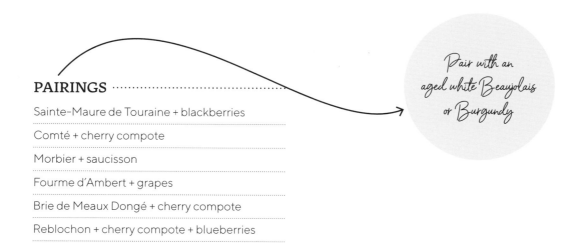

Pair with an aged white Beaujolais or Burgundy

Spanish Tapas Board

Take tapas to the next level with this cheese and charcuterie platter that incorporates some of the best of Spanish flavours into one party-ready spread. We've chosen five incredible Spanish cheeses and paired them with classic chorizo, padrón peppers and spicy olives. With lots of flavour-packed accompaniments, you might need a siesta after this mouthwatering feast. Manchego and quince is a flavour pairing as timeless and perfect as Romeo and Juliet, but do give the Picos blue and chorizo a try: with fruity, sweet, spicy, milky, fatty cheese notes in common, they are a match made in heaven.

COMPONENTS

Cheese
200g (7oz) vintage Manchego
250g (9oz) Cañarejal Cremoso
160g (5¾oz) La Retorta
100g (3½oz) Monte Enebro goat's cheese
100g (3½oz) Valdeón Picos blue

Meat
100g (3½oz) sliced rustic chorizo morcón

Accompaniments
100g (3½oz) spicy Spanish pitted green olives
30g (1oz) dried figs
100g (3½oz) fig and almond cake
1 fresh orange
50g (1¾oz) quince paste
40g (1½oz) jarred marinated artichoke hearts
40g (1½oz) spicy fried broad (fava) beans
100g (3½oz) cashews
50g (1¾oz) salted Marcona almonds

For the fried padrón peppers
200g (7oz) padrón peppers
Spanish olive oil, for drizzling
flaked sea salt

Bread and crackers
30g (1oz) olive oil crackers

PREP

Make the fried padrón peppers
Fry the padrón peppers in a hot dry pan over a high heat for a couple of minutes until starting to char, blister and soften slightly. Remove from the heat, drizzle with Spanish olive oil and sprinkle with salt.

Cut the Manchego into triangles and cut the tops off the Cañarejal Cremoso and La Retorta. Halve the Valdeón Picos blue lengthways. Slice the Monte Enebro into neat rounds.
 Place the olives in a ramekin. Cut the quince paste into the same-size triangles as the Manchego. Slice the dried figs, the fig and almond cake and the orange.

ASSEMBLE

Place the Cañarejal Cremoso and La Retorta on the board, one at the top and one on the middle left. Stack the crackers next to the Cañarejal Cremoso. Arrange two stacks of Manchego triangles at either end of the board, placing triangles of quince paste in between each piece of the stack nearest the board handle. Place the Valdeón Picos blue on either side of the Manchego in the bottom right corner then add the Monte Enebro rounds in the bottom left corner. Fill in all the gaps with the bowl of olives, fried padrón peppers, chorizo, artichokes, spicy fried broad beans (fava), nuts, dried figs, fig and almond cake and orange slices.

Pair with Rioja

PAIRINGS

Manchego + quince paste + spicy broad (fava) beans

Cañarejal Cremoso + marinated artichokes + cashews

La Retorta + dried figs + marinated artichokes

Monte Enebro goat's cheese + marinated artichokes

Valdeón Picos blue + chorizo morcón

The Caprese Board

Caprese salad – a combination of mozzarella, tomatoes and basil – is a dish so gloriously simple, yet it instantly transports you to sunny Capri. This is a board to make when tomatoes are in season and at their best — you should be able to smell them before you see them. This happens to be my favourite cheeseboard; it's easy to put together, delicious and beautiful. Add your own touch of homemade flair to this mouthwatering plate by loading it up with fresh produce, homemade pesto or your own favourite Italian treats. I love to pair a slightly bitter Negroni with the board as the fresh clean flavours cut through the creaminess of the cheese, and marry together with the other sweet, savoury and salty notes.

COMPONENTS

Cheese
80g (2¾oz) freshly grated
   Parmesan
2 x 250g (9oz) burrata balls
300g (10½oz) mozzarella
   bocconcini

Meat
150g (5½oz) sliced Italian salami

Accompaniments
3 beef (beefsteak) tomatoes
250g (9oz) cherry tomatoes
2 Roma tomatoes
1 Campari tomato
150g (5½oz) raspberries
100g (3½oz) toasted salted
   almonds
4 tbsp olive oil

For the pesto
150g (5½oz) fresh basil leaves
3 garlic cloves, peeled
3 tbsp pine nuts
1½ tbsp olive oil
flaked sea salt and freshly
   ground black pepper

Bread and crackers
1 loaf crusty ciabatta bread
180g (6¼oz) fennel crackers

Garnish
200g (7oz) fresh basil, so much
   basil!
50g (1¾oz) micro basil
100g (3½oz) pine nuts

PREP

Make the pesto
Place the basil, garlic, pine nuts and Parmesan in the bowl of a food processor. Blitz, then, with the motor running, add the olive oil in a slow, steady stream until everything is well blended. Season to taste with salt and pepper.

Leave two of the largest tomatoes whole and a few whole cherry tomatoes, and cut the rest of the tomatoes into slices or halves. Slice the loaf of ciabatta.

ASSEMBLE

Place a layer of basil leaves on the plate. Arrange the burrata over the basil leaves with the two whole beef tomatoes, then arrange the mozzarella bocconcini around the plate. Start adding the different kinds of tomatoes, mixing the different varieties together. Fold each slice of salami to create a triangle shape and lay in a line on the plate, between the cheese and tomatoes. Keep adding tomatoes – more is more when it comes to Caprese! Add the raspberries and some almonds here and there and drizzle lightly with olive oil.

   Finish with the micro basil leaves and pine nuts. Serve with the ciabatta bread and fennel crackers alongside.

Negroni or oaky Chardonnay

PAIRINGS

Burrata + beef tomatoes + pesto

Mozzarella bocconcini + Campari tomatoes + basil

Mozzarella bocconcini + Roma tomatoes + salami + pine nuts

Paneer Platter

This isn't your run-of-the-mill cheeseboard. It features an array of vibrant colours, incredible perfumes and aromatic spices, and encompasses lots of diverse textures and bold flavours, serving up some unexpected pairings – Brie and mango chutney might sound unusual but it is truly a match made in heaven. This platter is great to eat and fun to make. With such big flavours, I have steered away from a wine pairing and instead gone for a refreshing gin and tonic to cleanse the palette as you work your way through each bite and pairing.

COMPONENTS

Cheese
100g (3½oz) paneer
100g (3½oz) small soft goat's cheese (I like Banon)
150g (5½oz) mini Brie

For the paneer skewers
150g (5½oz) natural yogurt
3 tbsp harissa paste
4 limes, 3 juiced and 1 cut into wedges
2 small red onions, cut into 2cm (1in) chunks
flaked sea salt and freshly ground black pepper

Accompaniments
50g (1¾oz) mango chutney
30g (1oz) lime pickle
80g (2¾oz) masala nuts
50g (1¾oz) raita
100g (3½oz) roasted chickpeas (page 131)
3 large fresh figs
1 gold kiwi
1 green kiwi
50g (1¾oz) tandoori mix

Bread and crackers
2 coriander naan bread
6 mini pappadums

Garnish
30g (1oz) coriander (cilantro)

PREP

Make the paneer skewers
Heat the grill to high. Cut the paneer into 3cm (1¼in) pieces. Mix the yogurt in a medium bowl with the harissa paste, 1 tablespoon of the lime juice and some salt and pepper. Add the paneer and stir gently to coat. Thread the paneer onto 5 metal skewers, alternating with onion, then place on a baking tray lined with foil. Grill (broil) the skewers for 10 minutes, turning halfway through, until golden brown.

Cut the goat's cheese into wedges.
    Put the mango chutney and lime pickle in two separate small bowls or ramekins. Place the masala nuts and raita into two more bowls. Pour the roasted chickpeas into a final bowl.
    Cut the figs (some sliced, some quartered) and halve the kiwis.
    Cut the naan into triangles.

ASSEMBLE

Place the ramekins of lime pickle, mango chutney, masala nuts, raita and roasted chickpeas on or near the board, then place the mini pappadums and naan triangles on a separate plate. Place the mini Brie at the top of the board and the small soft goat's cheese at the bottom of the board, placing the paneer skewers next to the goat's cheese. Scatter the tandoori mix around the board and lay the kiwi halves near the Brie. Garnish with coriander (cilantro).

Pair with a gin & tonic or Cobra Premium lager

PAIRINGS

Paneer + lime pickle + kiwi

Soft goat's cheese + fresh figs

Brie + mango chutney

The Smörgåsbord

The classic Scandinavian concept of a smörgåsbord comprises
a mixture of hot and cold dishes and the scale borders almost on
a buffet. This platter has to be the most exquisite way to serve
a feast of colour, flavour and goodness to a crowd. It features an
assortment of good cheese, pickled vegetables, caviar (or fish roe)
and salmon with crispbread slices and rye bread. Serve it
alongside traditional schnapps or aquavit, but if you prefer a
lower ABV a Sancerre will stand up nicely to the range of flavours
mingling happily on this board. A smörgåsbord would not be
complete without traditional cheese varieties such as brown
Norwegian Gjetost and Jarlsberg: these cheeses complement the
fish flavours and the freshness of the pickles.

COMPONENTS ·······································

Cheese
200g (7oz) cottage cheese
300g (10½oz) Jarlsberg
150g (5½oz) goat's milk Gouda
100g (3½oz) Gjetost

Fish
10g (¼oz) salmon caviar or roe,
  optional
50g (1¾oz) sliced smoked salmon
2 pieces cooked salmon fillet

Accompaniments
750g (1lb 10oz) new potatoes
3 eggs
6 cooked quail eggs
130g (4½oz) pickled red cabbage
7 radishes
1 head of chicory (Belgian endive)
20g (¾oz) Gin-Pickled
  Cucumbers (page 165)
20g (¾oz) cornichons
1 lemon
30g (1oz) rocket (arugula)

For the cottage cheese dip
1 spring onion (scallion)
1 heaped tbsp fresh dill
squeeze of lemon juice
flaked sea salt and freshly
  ground black pepper

Bread and crackers
200g (7oz) seeded crackers
4 slices of rye bread

Garnish
50g (1¾oz) dill
1 tbsp capers

PREP

Make the cottage cheese dip
Thinly slice the spring onion (scallion) and roughly chop the dill. Mix with the cottage cheese and lemon juice in a bowl and season to taste with salt and pepper.

Cook the new potatoes in a saucepan of boiling salted water until tender, then drain.

Cook the hen's eggs in a saucepan of boiling water for 7 minutes, until hard boiled, then cool under cold running water, peel off the shells and halve the eggs. Halve the cooked quail's eggs.

Put the cottage cheese dip, pickled cabbage and salmon caviar or roe (if using) into separate bowls or ramekins.

Slice the Jarlsberg in half, so that you have two wedges, then cut the Gouda into triangles. Using your cheese plane, cut the Gjetost into neat triangles.

Thinly slice the radishes, using a mandoline if you have one, and separate the chicory leaves. Halve the lemon and then thinly slice it.

Lightly crush half of the cooked potatoes.

ASSEMBLE

Grab the largest chopping board or platter you have and get creative. Using the full rainbow of colours and layering up the variety of flavours, build the platter, starting by placing the bowls or ramekins across the board, leaving plenty of room in between each one. Place the Jarlsberg halves on the right of the board (arranging the board with it placed horizontally in front of you) and the Gouda and Gjetost triangles in separate piles or shingled layers near the centre of the board. Place the pickles, radishes, crispbread and rye bread and chicory around the edge of the board and finish off by adding the fish (flaking the cooked salmon), rocket (arugula), potatoes, lemon slices and halved eggs. Finally, fill the gaps with dill sprigs and sprinkle over the capers.

Pairs well with schnapps, aquavit or Sancerre

PAIRINGS

Cottage cheese dip + caviar + smoked salmon

Jarlsberg + gin-pickled cucumber

Goat's milk Gouda + pickled red cabbage

Gjetost + potato + cornichons

123

Cinco de Mayo Board

This Mexican cheeseboard is in the spirit of Cinco de Mayo, a festival that celebrates the Mexican victory over the French army, which has at its heart the most amazing food. Cheese is an important part of Mexican culinary culture, adding a salty, savoury dimension to tacos and many other dishes. This board includes the best Mexican cheese, plenty of dips, tasty bites and my very own cheese taco shells that are a family favourite: your Taco Tuesday is about to get a serious upgrade with these crispy cheese shells. Whilst it's best to use my choice of Mexican cheeses, I have also suggested easy-to-buy substitutes.

If you're not familiar with mezcal, it's like tequila's older, smoky sibling. For the best flavour experience, serve it neat for sipping, or as the base of a simple cocktail. It's a great match for the lively, fresh flavours going on in this platter.

PREP

Make the pico de gallo
Place the tomatoes, red onion, avocado, jalapeño pepper and garlic into a large bowl and stir to combine. Sprinkle over the coriander (cilantro) and add the lime juice then mix. Season with salt to taste.

Make the cheese taco shells
Grate the Red Leicester cheese. Place two tall glasses of equal height on the work surface to use to support each end of a spatula or wooden spoon, which you will hang the cheese tacos on.

Preheat a large non-stick frying pan (skillet) over a medium-low heat. Add a handful of the grated Red Leicester and spread it into a circle using the back of a measuring cup or spoon.

Cook for 3 minutes, or until uniformly melted and just beginning to turn golden brown then turn off the heat and let it cool briefly. Flip and let it cook in the residual heat for 1 more minute. While still warm, carefully pick up the cheese circle and drape it over the suspended spoon or spatula so it is hanging upside down. A few minutes of cooling will turn it into a taco shell! Repeat, to make eight cheese taco shells then place inside the hard corn taco shells.

COMPONENTS

Cheese
400g (14oz) Red Leicester
470g (16½oz) Parmesan, grated
100g (3½oz) Chihuahua cheese
100g (3½oz) Oaxaca cheese (quesillo)
200g (7oz) queso fresco

Meat
100g (3½oz) Mexican chorizo

Accompaniments
1 tsp olive oil
2 ripe avocados
100g (3½oz) shop-bought salsa
200g (7oz) homemade guacamole (page 162)
200g (7oz) soured cream
handful of crisp lettuce leaves

For the pico de gallo
5 tomatoes, diced
¼ red onion diced
1 ripe avocado, stoned, peeled and diced
½ large jalapeño pepper, diced
1 garlic clove, crushed
100g (3½oz) coriander (cilantro), chopped
2 tbsp lime juice
flaked sea salt

For the elote (Mexican street corn)
3 corn on the cob
50g (1¾oz) mayonnaise
2 tsp chilli powder
pinch of cumin
bunch of coriander (cilantro), freshly chopped

Bread and crackers
8 hard corn taco shells
300g (10½oz) tortilla chips

Garnish
5 limes, cut into wedges
handful of fresh coriander (cilantro)

Make the elote (Mexican street corn)

Preheat the grill (broiler) to medium-high or place a griddle pan over a medium-high heat. Put the corn under the grill or in the griddle pan and cook for a few minutes until it begins to brown, then turn and repeat until the corn is lightly charred all over – about 10 minutes cooking time in total.

In a small bowl, mix together the mayonnaise, chilli powder, cumin, 70g (2½oz) of the Parmesan and coriander (cilantro). Brush the mixture over the corn and sprinkle with more chilli and coriander (cilanto). Serve warm with lime wedges.

Cut the Chihuahua cheese into neat triangles. Grate half of the Oaxaca cheese and the Parmesan. Crumble all of the queso fresco.

Slice the chorizo into 5mm (¼in)-thick discs. Heat the teaspoon of oil in a medium frying pan (skillet) over a medium heat. Add the sliced chorizo and cook for 10 minutes, turning the slices after 5 minutes, until browned and crisp. Divide between the taco shells and top with some guacamole, soured cream and a sprinkle of pico de gallo.

Halve and stone the avocados (keeping the skin on). Place a griddle pan over a high heat and once hot, add the avocados, flesh-side down, and cook until griddle lines appear. Remove from the pan and set aside.

Place the salsa, guacamole, elote and pico de gallo into separate bowls or ramekins.

Cut the limes into wedges and shred the lettuce leaves.

ASSEMBLE

Lay the tacos along the length of the board and place the dishes of guacamole, pico de gallo and elote on the board. Sprinkle the grated Parmesan, Oaxaca and queso fresco over the tacos. Place the Chihuahua and remaining Oaxaca at opposite ends of the board, so that there's plenty of space in between each element. Fill in the gaps with the grilled avocados, shredded lettuce, tortilla chips, lime wedges and half of the bunch of coriander (cilantro). The board should be vibrant and overflowing. Finish by scattering the remaining coriander sprigs over the tacos.

Pairs with mezcal – try my Paloma cocktail on page 93, substituting the tequila for mezcal

PAIRINGS

Red Leicester + tacos + guacamole

Parmesan + elote + pico de gallo

Chihuahua cheese + salsa

Oaxaca cheese + Mexican chorizo

Queso fresco + pico de gallo

127

Caribbean Grill-out Cheeseboard

Board Style: Wooden tapas board
Serves: 10

This tropical cheeseboard is bursting with fun flavours, bright fruits and vivid colours. It's a showstopping party board for any gathering. Featuring some of the best and brightest cheeses, plus a whole handful of mouthwatering accompaniments, including plenty of fresh fruits, it's a little taste of paradise all served on banana leaves. The Gruyère and passion fruit pairing may sound unexpected but the beautiful nutty flavour of the cheese pairs perfectly with the tropical fruit; mozzarella is mild and sweet so works really well with these flavours too. Chow is a popular on-the-go snack that hails from Trinidad and is made with fresh fruit, onion and garlic, seasoned with chilli. Alongside this brilliant combination of fresh, fruity and spicy ingredients, I've suggested serving rum punch; the ideal match for relaxing with friends around this most joyful platter.

PREP

Make the mango and cucumber chow
Combine the lime juice, garlic, scotch bonnet and red onion in a bowl. Add the mango, cucumber, pineapple, salt and a pinch of black pepper and mix well. Cover and leave in the fridge for 1½ hours. Half an hour before you're ready to serve, remove from the fridge so it has a chance to come to room temperature.

Make the grilled pineapple
Halve the pineapple lengthways, removing the top and the tough core. Cut each half into thin wedges, skin on. Heat a griddle pan over a medium heat. Toss the pineapple in a bowl with the lime juice and dark brown sugar, making sure the pineapple pieces are evenly coated. Grill the pineapple until golden brown, flipping the pieces halfway through.

Make the garlicky plantain
Heat the oil in a large saucepan over a medium heat. Add the plantain rounds and fry. Once they soften and become golden brown, flip them over and cook on the other side. This will take 4–6 minutes. Transfer to kitchen paper (paper towels) to remove excess oil.

Add the garlic to the pan and place over a medium-high heat. Fry the plantains again, turning them once, for 6–8 minutes until deep golden brown. Transfer to fresh pieces of kitchen paper (paper towels) to drain; sprinkle with salt.

COMPONENTS

Cheese
200g (7oz) mozzarella bocconcini
300g (10½oz) 24-month Gruyère
150g (5½oz) mini Brie

Meat
40g (1½oz) sliced prosciutto

Accompaniments
1 small watermelon
3 dragon fruit (pitaya)
4 passion fruit
4 star fruit
1 honeydew melon
2 coconuts
200g (7oz) Hot Peach Pickle
   (page 161)
2 kumquats
4 physalis (cape gooseberries)
2 persimmons
2 mangoes
4 scotch bonnet chillies
100g (3½oz) spicy Marcona
   almonds

For the mango and cucumber chow
2½ tbsp lime juice
2 garlic cloves, finely grated
1 scotch bonnet chilli
1 large red onion, thinly sliced
   into rings
2 ripe but firm mangoes, peeled,
   stoned and cubed
1 cucumber, cubed
¼ small pineapple, cubed
freshly ground black pepper
1 tsp flaked sea salt
½ empty pineapple shell

For the grilled pineapple
2 small pineapples
2 tbsp lime juice
2 tbsp dark brown sugar

For the garlicky plantains

2 tbsp olive oil
2 large ripe plantains, cut into
    bite-sized rounds
1 garlic clove, crushed
flaked sea salt, to taste

For the roasted chickpeas

400g (14oz) tin chickpeas,
    drained
1 tsp olive oil
2 tsp smoked paprika
1 tsp freshly ground black pepper
1 tsp flaked sea salt

Garnish

2 large banana leaves
1 pallet hibiscus flowers
    (optional)
1 coconut shell
4 limes, cut into wedges
2 mint sprigs, leaves stripped
    from the stems

Make the roasted chickpeas

Preheat the oven to 200°C (400°F/Gas Mark 6). Put the chickpeas in a large bowl, add the oil, smoked paprika, salt and pepper and toss to coat well. Tip onto a baking tray and roast in the oven for 35 minutes, stirring halfway through so they dry out evenly and are crunchy.

Cut the watermelon into triangle wedges. Halve the dragon fruit and passion fruit. Slice the star fruit. Cut the honeydew melon into wedges, removing the seeds, and wrap some of the wedges with prosciutto.

Cut one of the coconuts into cubes, keeping the other one whole for the board.

Place the peach pickle and mozzarella bocconcini into separate bowls or ramekins. Cut the Gruyère into long triangles.

Fill the empty pineapple shell with the mango and cucumber chow and cut the limes into wedges. Cut half the top off the Brie.

ASSEMBLE

Lay the banana leaves on a large cheeseboard so you can move them if needs be. Place the chow-filled pineapple at the bottom right of the board. Shingle the Gruyère triangles on the middle of the board, with the Brie to the left. Place the ramekin of mozzarella to the right of the Gruyère triangles, and shingle the grilled pineapple and plantain to the right of the board, placing the bowl of peach pickle nearby. Fill the rest of the board with the prepared fruits and prosciutto-wrapped melon as desired, and fill the gaps with the almonds and cubed coconut. Garnish the board with the hibiscus flowers (if using) and coconut shell, and add lime wedges to finish. Sprinkle the mint leaves over the bowl of mozzarella bocconcini.

Pairs with a rum punch

PAIRINGS

Mozzarella + Hot Peach Pickle + grilled pineapple

Gruyère + passion fruit

Brie + prosciutto + melon

131

SHOWSTOPPER
BOARDS

Every Day I'm Trufflin'

The rich umami of rare and aromatic black truffles is a truly unique flavour and are a luxurious addition to any dish. And the best way of eating truffles of all is... truffles in cheese. This decadent board is a pure celebration of truffle-studded cheeses, including Burrata, Gouda and Brie. From creamy to crumbly and mild to wild, these cheeses burst with fragrant flavour. This is a great board to enjoy in autumn or winter when the truffles are at their best.

The rich truffle Brie is the star of the cheeseboard with the decadent truffle flavour present in each bite. It makes the perfect companion to a glass of champagne and is ideal for a special occasion or treat.

COMPONENTS

Cheese
100g (3½oz) black truffle-infused Gouda
300g (10½oz) truffle Brie
150g (5½oz) burrata ball
150g (5½oz) cream cheese
200g (7oz) black summer truffle Pecorino

Meat
50g (1¾oz) sliced truffle-infused salami
100g (3½oz) sliced prosciutto di Parma

Accompaniments
30g (1oz) runny honey
3 fresh figs
100g (3½oz) cherries
stem of vine cherry tomatoes
50g (1¾oz) dried apricots
20g (¾oz) olive oil
20g (¾oz) piece of fresh black truffle

Bread and crackers
100g (3½oz) Linguette

Garnish
bunch of oregano
2 Sicilian lemons

PREP

Cut the Gouda into thin triangles and the truffle Brie in half to make 2 wedges. Place the burrata in a shallow, small bowl and put the cream cheese into a ramekin or bowl. Put the honey in a small bowl or ramekin. Cut a few slices from one of the Sicilian lemons and cut one of the figs in half.

ASSEMBLE

Put the bowls or ramekins of burrata, cream cheese and honey on the board, with the burrata near the top and the cream cheese towards the centre with the honey next to it. Place the Brie wedges on the left side of the board. Place the whole Pecorino chunk next to it and arrange the Gouda triangles to the right, next to the cream cheese. Surround the bowl of burrata with fans of salami and lemon slices. Place the prosciutto di Parma and Linguette at the bottom of the board. Fill in the gaps with the cherries, cherry tomatoes, dried apricots and fresh figs. Garnish the board with oregano. For a final flourish, drizzle olive oil on the burrata and add a shaving of fresh truffle over the burrata and cream cheese: be generous!

Pair with Champagne & Pinot Noir

PAIRINGS

Truffle-infused Gouda + dried apricots

Truffle Brie + honey

Burrata + olive oil + fresh truffle

Cream cheese + fresh truffle + cherries

Black summer truffle Pecorino + Linguette

Antipasto Board

Antipasto is traditionally the opener to a formal Italian meal. Whether you're snacking on olives with a glass of crisp white wine or picking at some chunks of Parmigiano-Reggiano with some silky slices of prosciutto, you can't go wrong with a savoury/ sweet snack before a classic Mediterranean meal. It would not be a Mediterranean dining experience if you didn't enjoy this board with a Pinot Grigio. This dry wine has aromatic, fruity flavours that really helps make the Parmigiano-Reggiano come alive.

COMPONENTS

Cheese
150g (5½oz) 24-month Parmigiano-Reggiano
200g (7oz) aged Provolone del Monaco
200g (7oz) Taleggio
150g (5½oz) Gorgonzola dolce
100g (3½oz) mozzarella balls marinated in olive oil and oregano

Meat and fish
300g (10½oz) large whole salami
50g (1¾oz) tin of anchovy fillets in oil
250g (9oz) tin of Italian sardines
50g (1¾oz) sliced prosciutto
30g (1oz) sliced salami
50g (1¾oz) Italian dry salami

Accompaniments
40g (1½oz) marinated artichoke hearts
50g (1¾oz) marinated mushrooms
20g (¾oz) roasted red (bell) peppers

50g (1¾oz) marinated olives in olive oil
20g (¾oz) Kalamata olives
20g (¾oz) green olive tapenade
40g (1½oz) pesto
4 ripe peaches
large bunch of green grapes
8 cherry tomatoes on the vine
handful of roasted salted almonds

Bread and crackers
½ baguette
5–8 Gristini

Garnish
20g (¾oz) rocket (arugula)

PREP

Crumble off a few pieces of the Parmigiano-Reggiano and keep the rest intact. Cut a piece from the aged Provolone, keep the Taleggio whole and cut a few wedges from the Gorgonzola dolce.

Slice some of the baguette.

Place the artichoke hearts, roasted peppers, both olives, tapenade and pesto into separate ramekins or bowls. Place the mozzarella balls in a ramekin or bowl. Open the tins of anchovies and sardines.

Halve one of the peaches and cut one of the halves into thin wedges.

ASSEMBLE

Start by putting the cheeses (including the ramekin or bowl of mozzarella balls) on the bottom half of the board, arranging them so they are an equal distance apart. Place the pesto ramekin near the mozzarella balls and place the other ramekins or bowls, and tins of fish, on the top half of the board. Fill in the gaps with the meats, marinated mushrooms, cherry tomatoes, peaches, grapes, almonds and Grissini. Garnish the board with rocket (arugula). Serve with the baguette on the side.

Goes well with Pinot Grigio, Sangiovese di Romagna or Prosecco

PAIRINGS

Marinated mozzarella + prosciutto + tomatoes

24-month Parmigiano-Reggiano + salami

Aged Provolone + marinated mushrooms + salami

Taleggio + peaches + prosciutto

Gorgonzola dolce + roasted almonds

139

Farmers' Market Rainbow Board

Board Style: Large wooden chopping board
Serves: 8–10

One of the reasons I love a farmers' market so much is the wonderful array of colourful produce – a treat for your eyes and your taste buds! This board celebrates the best of the market: from crisp fresh veggies and juicy fruits to rich cheeses and salty meats. Try a rainbow of 12 cheeses paired with the best market produce. Sample apricot and Brie or blackberries and ash goat's cheese or even Old Amsterdam Gouda with watermelon radish. This board has something for everyone and is the perfect party centrepiece. Remember to follow the red, orange, yellow, green, blue, indigo and violet pattern to achieve the full rainbow affect.

PREP

Cut the Cornish Yarg into cubes, leaving the rind on, and cut the top off the Snowdonia Green Thunder, leaving the green wax on. Dice the Jarlsberg and the mature Cheddar. Warm through the honey, then place it in a small jar or ramekin. Place the raspbery jam and beetroot hummus into two additional (separate) ramekins or bowls.

    Cut both colours of carrot into batons and halve some of the yelllow peppers. Halve some of the cherry tomatoes and thinly slice the cucumbers, lime, candy-stripe beetroot and radish. Halve the strawberries lengthways, halve the pomegranate, papaya and apricot, and slice the orange. Quarter one of the figs.

    'Hedgehog' the mango half by cutting a crosshatch pattern in the flesh, cutting all the way through the flesh but not through the skin. Invert it and expose the cubes by pressing the flesh out from the skin side.

ASSEMBLE

With this board, the assembly is really important. Use a large rectangle board and, starting from the top-right corner, work your way down to the bottom-left, placing the components above in this colour order: red, orange, yellow, green, blue, and indigo/violet. Garnish the green ingredients with the basil, rosemary and mint and the rest of the board with edible flowers to match the colours of the other components on the board.

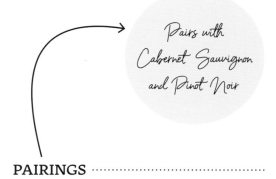

Pairs with Cabernet Sauvignon and Pinot Noir

PAIRINGS

Old Amsterdam + strwberries + mint

Shropshire Blue + dried apricots

Red Leicester + green grapes

Munster + red grapes

Jarlsberg + dried apricots

Mature Cheddar + red grapes

Brie + raspberries

Cornish Yarg + strawberries

Snowdonia Green Thunder + honey

Colston Bassett Stilton + blueberries

Roquefort + raspberries

Ash pyramid goat's cheese + blueberries + raspberries

COMPONENTS ···

Cheese

ORANGE:
100g (3½oz) Old Amsterdam
100g (3½oz) Shropshire Blue
50g (1¾oz) Red Leicester
30g (1oz) Munster

YELLOW:
150g (5½oz) Jarlsberg
150g (5½oz) mature Cheddar
90g (3¼oz) Brie

GREEN:
100g (3½oz) Cornish Yarg
200g (7oz) Snowdonia Green Thunder

BLUE:
100g (3½oz) Colston Bassett Stilton
50g (1¾oz) Roquefort
140g (5oz) ash pyramid goat's cheese

Meat

30g (1oz) sliced salami
30g (1oz) sliced bresaola

Accompaniments

WHITE:
handful of mini breadsticks

RED:
100g (3½oz) strawberries
130g (4½oz) raspberries
2 stalks of redcurrants
1 pomegranate
small bunch of red grapes
20g (¾oz) raspberry jam
30g (1oz) Negroni Chutney (page 162)

ORANGE:
1 orange
handful of orange cherry tomatoes
3 orange carrots
½ papaya
handful of dried apricots
1 fresh apricot
30g (1oz) runny honey

YELLOW:
4 small yellow peppers
½ mango
½ passion fruit

GREEN:
½ cucumber
large bunch of green grapes
10g (⅓oz) sweet young peas in their pods
1 lime

BLUE:
150g (5½oz) blueberries
handful of blackberries
large bunch of black grapes

INDIGO/VIOLET:
7 fresh figs
handful of dark cherries
2 purple carrots
2 plums
100g (3½oz) beetroot crackers
2 candy-stripe beetroot (beets)
50g (1¾oz) Beetroot Hummus (page 163)
1 watermelon radish

Garnish

edible flowers in a range of colours
30g (1oz) basil leaves
30g (1oz) rosemary
handful of mint leaves

Chocolate and Cheese Heaven

This delightfully decadent board puts the unlikely pairing of cheese and chocolate at its centre. Chocolate and blue cheese work surprisingly well together as the chocolate mellows and balances out the strong flavor of the cheese. Match the 70% dark chocolate bar with the strong Cheddar and note how the fruity notes of the chocolate are enhanced. The rich red notes of the fruit on the board complement the dark chocolate and creamy cheese to make a chic centrepiece to a small party or gathering.

COMPONENTS

Cheese
250g (9oz) vintage Cheddar
150g (5½oz) Bleu d'Auvergne
80g (2¾oz) Gorgonzola dolce
200g (7oz) Gouda
150g (5½oz) Camembert

Accompaniments
250g (9oz) strawberries
100g (3½oz) dark chocolate (70% cocoa solids)
100g (3½oz) milk chocolate
30g (1oz) peach compote

120g (4¼oz) fig and almond cake
handful of raspberries
handful of cherries
100g (3½oz) chocolate truffles
10 chocolate-covered cherries
4 white chocolate sticks
handful of roasted hazelnuts
30g (1oz) Marcona almonds

Garnish
sprig of mint leaves

PREP

Crumble some of the vintage Cheddar into chunks, leaving the rest intact, and cut the Bleu d'Auvergne and Gorgonzola dolce into triangles. Cut some of the Gouda into long, thin triangles.

Halve some of the strawberries and break all the chocolate into bite-sized chunks, leaving a few large bits.

Place the peach compote in a small jar or ramekin. Slice the fig and almond cake.

ASSEMBLE

Place the Camembert on the top left of the plate or platter and top it with some fruit and a few mint leaves. Put the jar or ramekin of peach compote in the centre of the plate or platter. Arrange the remaining cheeses around the plate or platter, leaving room in between each so there's space for the accompaniments.

Arrange the fruit in piles, then fill in the gaps with the chocolate pieces, truffles and nuts.

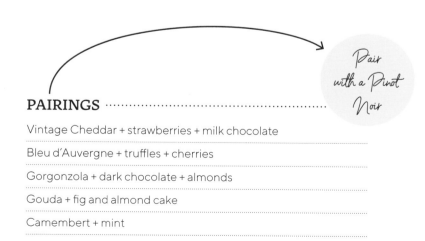

Pair with a Pinot Noir

PAIRINGS

Vintage Cheddar + strawberries + milk chocolate

Bleu d'Auvergne + truffles + cherries

Gorgonzola + dark chocolate + almonds

Gouda + fig and almond cake

Camembert + mint

The Birthday Board

Presenting the most decadent celebration of all things cheese. There is no better way to celebrate a birthday than a vast amount of cheese and wine. This is the perfect way to say happy birthday to a cheese lover: it features nothing less than a tower of cheese and is not just visually impressive but the flavours on this board are stunning. The cheeses are guaranteed crowd winners: Brillat-Savarin is pure, heavenly indulgence, creamy goat's Brie, rich Crottin de Chavignol and I've included some perennial favourites too, Manchego and Brie!

COMPONENTS

Cheese
180g (6½oz) Manchego
1kg (2lb 3oz) Brie
250g (9oz) Camembert
250g (9oz) goat's Brie
1kg (2lb 4oz) Brillat-Savarin
60g (2oz) Crottin de Chavignol

Meat
120g (4¼oz) sliced salami

Accompaniments
30g (1oz) piece of honeycomb
30g (1oz) honey
30g (1oz) bacon jam
3 large bunches of mixed grapes

1 apple
20g (¾oz) blueberries
40g (1½oz) raspberries
40g (1½oz) redcurrants
8 large fresh figs

Bread and crackers
100g (3½oz) sourdough crackers

Garnish
candles
1 'Happy Birthday' sign (optional)
bunch of white roses
20g (¾oz) rosemary

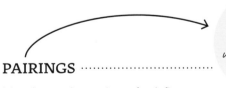

Goes perfectly with Champagne

PAIRINGS

Manchego + bacon jam + fresh figs

Brie + bacon jam

Brillat-Savarin + blueberries + rosemary

Camembert + honeycomb + grapes

Goat's Brie + fresh figs + apple

Crottin de Chavignol + apple + salami

PREP

Cut the Manchego into small triangles. Unlike other boards, keep the cheeses in the fridge right up until you assemble the board.
Place the honeycomb , honey and bacon jam in separate ramekins.
Quarter the figs and thinly slice the apple.

ASSEMBLE

Arrange the cheese tower on the right-hand side of the board. Starting with the first layer and working up, place the Brie directly on the board, then place the Brillat-Savarin on top, followed by the Camembert and the goat's Brie, and, at the very top, the Crottin de Chavignol. If you are planning on keeping the cheese out for a while, place slim pieces of card cut to the shape of the cheeses between each layer – this helps to keep the shape of the cheese. Fill the rest of the board with all of the delicious accompaniments that go with the cheese tower: fan the Manchego triangles down the right side, then the salami in neat folds; place the ramekins of honeycomb, honey and bacon jam; then fill in the gaps with crackers and fruit.

GARNISH

Place the candles and 'Happy Birthday' sign, if using, on the cheese tower, and down the left side of the tower place the edible flowers, then carry this on to the board below, adding rosemary to the accompaniments.

From the Sea

Seafood and cheese aren't a typical pairing — their respective light and subtle versus heavy and palate-dominating natures have often kept them apart – but here are some exceptions to that rule. This seacuterie board is sure to make a splash at your next dinner party and the flavour pairings not only bring the seafood to life, they will also make you think about cheese pairings in a completely new way. From baked Parmesan scallops to oysters with a classic mignonette sauce, have fun with your favourite seafood and accompanying bites. Serve this on a marble or metal board and place it in the fridge a few hours before assembling the board, so it is cold when serving.

COMPONENTS

Cheese
100g (3½oz) Parmesan
180g (6oz) cream cheese
2 150g (5½oz) burrata balls
200g (7oz) Gruyère
200g (7oz) Fourme d'Ambert
150g (5½oz) mini Brie

Fish and seafood
6 scallops in their shells
6 oysters
1 cooked lobster
8 slices of smoked salmon
5 cooked cocktail prawns
  (shrimp), shells and heads
  intact
20g (¾oz) pot of caviar

Accompaniments
20g (¾oz) Gin-Pickled
  Cucumbers (page 165)
1 tsp capers

For the mignonette sauce
1 small shallot, finely chopped
120ml (4fl oz/½ cup) red wine
  vinegar
½ tbsp crushed black
  peppercorns

For the Parmesan-baked scallops
100g (3½oz) salted butter
5 garlic cloves, crushed
handful of flat-leaf parsley, finely
  chopped
100g (3½oz/2 cups) fresh
  breadcrumbs
splash of dry white wine

Bread and crackers
1 baguette
16 blinis

Garnish
1 bag of crushed ice
30g (1oz) flat-leaf parsley
100g (3½oz) dill fronds

Goes well with a Pinot Grigio

PAIRINGS

Cream cheese + caviar + lemon

Burrata cream + smoked salmon

Gruyère + Gin-Pickled Cucumbers

Forme d'Ambert + Gin-Pickled Cucumbers

Brie + smoked salmon + Gin-Pickled Cucumbers

PREP

Make the mignonette sauce

Stir the shallot, red wine vinegar and crushed black peppercorns together in a small bowl. Chill until ready to serve.

Make the Parmesan-baked scallops

Preheat the oven to 250°C (500°F/highest Gas Mark). Rinse and dry the scallop shells and arrange them on a baking sheet. Make the garlic butter by melting the butter in a microwave or pan, then adding the crushed garlic and a handful of chopped parsley and mixing to combine. Put the scallops in a bowl, sprinkle the breadcrumbs over them, and toss to coat each one well with the crumbs. Place a teaspoon of garlic butter in each shell. Put three breaded scallops on top of the butter and sprinkle with any leftover breadcrumbs from the bottom of the bowl. Add a splash of wine, grate over the Parmesan and bake in the oven for 15–20 minutes, until the breadcrumbs are crispy and the butter is turning black around the edges of the shell. Let cool slightly before handling – the shells will be extremely hot

Prepare the oysters

Fill a round metal plate with crushed ice, to sit the oysters on. Shuck the oysters by wrapping a tea towel around your hand then holding an oyster with the pointed end facing out. Carefully wedge an oyster knife or long pointed knife into one side of the point and twist it with even force to open the oyster. Work your way around the top shell, disconnecting the muscle with the knife. Discard the top shell and gently run the knife along the bottom shell to release the oyster. Repeat with the remaining oysters then arrange them on the plate of crushed ice with the bowl of mignonette sauce in the centre.

Put the cream cheese in a small ramekin. Scoop out the middle of the burrata into a bowl. Cut the Gruyère into long batons. Crumble a little of the Fourme d'Ambert, leaving the rest intact.

Place the gin-pickled cucumber in a small ramekin. Put the mini Brie on a plate and cut out a triangle to expose the creamy interior. Slice the baguette.

ASSEMBLE

Place the dish of oysters on the right of your board and the lobster intact at the top, with some lobster pickers for retrieving the meat. Position the Fourme d'Ambert (intact and crumbled) just below the oyster dish. Place the ramekins and bowls of gin-pickled cucumbers, cream cheese and burrata cream throughout the board. Fan the Gruyère batons to the left of the middle of the board and arrange the prawns (shrimp) next to the Gruyère. Fold the salmon slices and place near the middle of the board, garnished with capers, and place the plate of Brie close by. Place the scallops on the board, making sure they are not too close to the cheese as they will still be hot. Fill in the gaps on the board with the rest of the accompaniments. Open the pot of caviar and place it near the Gruyère. Garnish the whole board with parsley and dill. Serve with the blinis.

151

The Pièce de Resistance: the grazing table

If you want your next party to look inviting and impressive, a cheese grazing table might be the answer. Simple, effective and most importantly, delicious!

What is it? A 'grazing table' is a tablescape filled with artfully arranged cheese, meats, crudités, as well as seasonal fruit, flowers, decorations and serving utensils and dishes. It's a relaxed way for you and your guests to mingle without actually cooking a formal meal. It is essentially a very largescale cheeseboard.

It's usually a table, but it can even be a large platter, wooden board, counter or just any large and flat surface. Food items aren't always contained on plates or bowls, but arranged artfully in piles that spill, overlap and intertwine into each other, so it doesn't just taste delicious, it looks delicious. The key thing to remember here is: organized chaos.

Here are some of my go-to tips to create the perfect grazing board.

1. PICK A THEME

Go wild with this, a grazing board can be adapted to any occasion, time of year, season or event. For example, a summer grazing board can be full of amazing fruit, vegetables and cheeses that are easily available and particularly delicious in the summer months. Summer dips, snacks and fresh salads, surrounded by fresh flowers, foliage and candles create a grazing paradise. Or a Christmas grazing table can include Christmas classic cheeses like Stilton and mature Cheddar, cold meats, festive red and green baubles and props like candles around the table.

2. CHOOSE YOUR CHEESES

They are the star of the show after all. When assembling a grazing table it is really nice to have a variety of cheeses: I recommend:

* one soft
* one fresh and mild
* one buttery and rich
* one semi-soft
* one smooth and nutty
* one strong and salty blue
* one creamy blue
* one hard, sharp
* one crunchy hard.

A wide range of cheeses is great because you are able to pair them with all the other produce on the table.

3. PRODUCE

Try to use seasonal, local produce where possible. Choose fresh vegetables, fruit, homemade dips and a mixture of breads, crackers and biscuits. Boards of salamis and cured meats, along with tinned and smoked fish all look great, and snacks, such as mini skewers, provide instant pre-made pairings. Make sure there's something for everyone.

4. GARNISHES GALORE

Flowers, herbs and foliage will add visual appeal to your grazing table. I like to include edible flowers to add colour and texture throughout the board. and these can be placed on top of all the foodie delights. Follow my guide on page 24 for suggestions of the best edible flowers to use.

5. CROCKERY

I LOVE a good bit of crockery and on a grazing table you need plenty of it. Muted and neutral-coloured plates, bowls, placemats and boards, are more versatile than brightly patterned serveware, and can be reused multiple times without feeling tired. Be sure to include plenty of cheese knifes, serving spoons and other cuttlery. Having a range of serving platters, ramekins and cake stands will add height and interest to your grazing table.

SET-UP TIP

Start with picking up a roll of greaseproof paper to lay out on the tabletop or counter that you are using for the grazing table. This will stop any staining of the table underneath. Be sure to use an appropriate size table for what you are serving. If the surface is too small, your guests won't be able to easily reach all of the food. If your table is too large, with lots of space around it, your feast will look underwhelming. Your grazing table should be a showstopper.

Use different sizes and shapes of crockery and serveware. Cake stands, marble, slate and wooden boards, mats, dishes and tiered stands will display your food at different heights and add a three dimensional feel to your table. This, in turn, will give it more visual appeal.

Make sure your table looks beautiful but inviting and accessible. The aim is to encourage your guests to dig in and enjoy the food, rathering than admiring a work of art.

Cut a bit from the whole cheese wheel, this will be more inviting and less intimidating when guests begin serving themselves. Try and serve your soft cheeses whole, this will help them last the length of the party.

Try to place food that pairs well together so for example grapes next to the Brie or figs next to the blue cheese.

RECIPES FOR THE BOARDS

My Perfect Piccalilli

A British cheeseboard staple, this tangy piccalilli is a must-have accompaniment. It's the perfect partner for a Cheshire cheese.

500g (1lb 2oz) cauliflower, broken into small florets
200g (7oz) courgettes (zucchini), cut into small chunks
150g (5½oz) green beans, trimmed and cut into small pieces
100g (3½oz) red onion, finely chopped
5cm (2in) piece of fennel, cut into 1cm (½in) pieces
2 tbsp flaked sea salt, plus a pinch extra for the vinegar
600ml (20fl oz/2½ cups) malt vinegar
3 tbsp English mustard powder
2 tbsp black or yellow mustard seeds
2 tsp cumin seeds
pinch of dried chilli flakes
4 tbsp plain (all-purpose) flour
1 tsp turmeric
200g (7oz/1 cup) caster (superfine) sugar

Toss all of the veggies in a large bowl with the 2 tablespoons of salt, cover and leave for 1 hour, then drain and rinse thoroughly under cold running water.

Put 100ml (3½fl oz/scant ½ cup) of the vinegar in a large bowl, then add the mustard powder, mustard seeds, cumin seeds, chilli flakes, flour and turmeric and mix to form a paste.

Heat the rest of the vinegar in a large saucepan over a medium heat, then add the sugar, and a pinch of salt. Stir until the sugar dissolves, then add the mustard and vinegar paste. Stir again and simmer for 5 minutes until it starts to thicken. Add the drained veggies and heat through for 1 minute, then remove from the heat.

Leave to cool then transfer into sterilised jars or containers.

My Tomato Chutney

The ideal tomato chutney, with just a hint of spice – a perfect pairing for a mature Cheddar cheese.

2 tsp cumin seeds
2 tsp coriander seeds
750g (1lb 10oz) ripe cherry tomatoes
1 onion, finely chopped
1 shallot, finely chopped
2 garlic cloves, crushed
2 large, mild red chillies (keep the seeds in if you like it spicy)
5cm (2in) piece of root ginger, peeled and grated
250ml (9fl oz/1 generous cup) white wine vinegar
300g (10½oz/1½ cups) soft light brown sugar
2 tsp soy sauce

Toast the cumin and coriander seeds in a small frying pan over a low heat for 1 minute, then crush in a pestle and mortar until finely ground.

Put the tomatoes, onion and shallot in a large saucepan with the garlic, chillies and grated ginger. Add the vinegar and sugar, bring to the boil, then simmer for 45 minutes until the mixture has reduced and thickened to a jam-like consistency. Stir in the soy sauce then decant into sterilised containers or jars and seal while hot, then allow to cool completely before eating.

Hot Peach Pickle

This pickle will add a spicy kick to your board and is the perfect contrast to cool and creamy goat's cheese.

700g (1lb 9oz) firm peaches
½ tbsp olive oil
1 red onion, thinly sliced
1 tbsp cumin seeds, toasted
1 tsp coriander seeds, toasted and lightly crushed
seeds from 10 green cardamom pods
200g (7oz/1 cup) soft light brown sugar
250ml (8fl oz/1 cup) cider vinegar
6 red chillies, deseeded and finely chopped
thumb-sized piece of root ginger, peeled and cut into
    fine matchsticks

First, peel the peaches. Prepare a pan or heatproof bowl of warm water and a separate bowl of iced water. Add the peaches and leave them to soak for about 1 minute, then transfer to the iced water. Once cooled, the peach skin should be very easy to pull away gently with your fingers. Stone the peaches and finely chop the flesh into cubes.

Heat the oil in a large saucepan over a medium heat, then add the onion and cook for a few minutes until soft but not brown. Add the spices and cook for a further 2 minutes, then add the rest of the ingredients. Stir to combine, then increase the heat and keep stirring until all of the sugar has dissolved. Reduce the heat and simmer for about 45 minutes, until most of the liquid has evaporated, the peaches have softened and the mixture has thickened. Pop into sterilised jars and seal once cooled. Store in a cool, dry place and use within 2 weeks.

Pear Compote

This French classic is a regular on my cheeseboards. The sweetness is a great pairing for the nuttiness in cheeses like Comté or Beaufort.

300g (10½oz) medium-sized ripe pears
2 tsp lemon juice
1 tsp caster (superfine) sugar
3 prunes, pitted and quartered
1 star anise
1 clove

Prepare the pears by peeling, coring and cubing them.

Place the cubed pears in a small saucepan with the lemon juice, sugar and 2 tablespoons of water. Bring to a simmer over a medium heat, stir, then reduce to a low heat.

Add the remaining ingredients, cover and cook for 20 minutes.

Remove the lid, stir and cook for another 10 minutes or until the liquid has reduced and the mixture has turned syrupy. Remove from the heat and discard the clove and star anise. Transfer into sterilised jars, seal and store in the fridge. The compote will keep for up to 5 days.

Negroni Chutney

This cocktail-in-a-jar chutney, which combines a fantastic drink and beautiful accompaniment, can help bring a cheeseboard to life. It's perfect with a sheep's cheese like Manchego.

2 oranges
1 lemon
½ grapefruit
320g (11¼oz/1½ cups) granulated sugar
1 tsp gin
200ml (7fl oz/scant 1 cup) Campari
1 tsp orange zest, plus extra to garnish
1 cinnamon stick

Cut the oranges, lemon and grapefruit into quarters then remove the cores and any seeds. Slice the fruit quarters into thin pieces to make small triangle shapes. Put them in a large bowl and fill it with water until the fruit is covered. Leave overnight.

Put the sugar, gin and Campari in a saucepan and stir over a low heat until the sugar has dissolved. Add the orange zest and cinnamon stick and cook gently over a medium heat until the mixture has reduced by half.

Pour the mixture into sterilised jars and leave it to cool completely, then seal.

Guacamole

There is nothing better than fresh guacamole and my recipe is super simple using easy-to-find ingredients and nice, ripe avocados. This is a great addition to any cheeseboard, particularly the Cinco de Mayo Board on page 126.

3 large, ripe avocados
2 medium tomatoes
1 red onion
juice of 1 lime
1 red chilli
bunch of coriander (cilantro), finely chopped
salt and freshly ground black pepper

Dice the avocado into large cubes and place in a medium bowl. Use a fork to mash the flesh so that it starts to form a paste but so that you still have some whole pieces of avocado – you don't want it to be too smooth.

Finely dice the tomatoes and red onion and stir into the avocado. Add the lime juice and mix well.

Season to taste with chilli, coriander, salt and pepper and then top with extra chilli and coriander to serve.

Beetroot Hummus

Hummus is my go-to dip and it is really great with cheese, but to add a bit of bite and colour to my boards, I love a beetroot hummus. Serve alongside feta and flatbread.

2 cooked beetroot (beet)
400g (14oz) tin chickpeas (garbanzos), drained
1 garlic clove
handful of fresh dill, finely chopped
3 tbsp tahini
½ tsp salt
1 tbsp olive oil
1 tsp ground cumin
grated zest and juice of 1 lemon

Put the beetroot (beets), chickpeas (garbanzos) and garlic into a blender and blitz for a minute until ground. Add the remaining ingredients and process until creamy.

The hummus should be a little grainy but if you'd like it smoother, then add more olive oil or tahini to taste. Refrigerate until ready to eat.

Boozy Pickles

These boozy pickles are bound to be a hit at your next cheese and wine party. The sweet and savoury pickles are soaked in tequila and preserved to create the perfect pickle. Serve with Gruyère.

500g (1lb 2oz) jar of large, whole pickles of your choice
70ml (2½fl oz/scant 5 tbsp) Blanco Tequila
5 chillies, thinly sliced (remove the seeds if you want less of a kick)

Remove 70ml (2½fl oz/scant 5 tbsp) pickle brine from the jar of pickles. Pour the tequila into the jar then add the chillies. Screw the lid on tightly, seal and shake thoroughly, so that the chillies are evenly distributed throughout the jar. Set aside for 30 minutes.

After 30 minutes, taste the pickle vinegar to check the spice level and if it is hot enough for you, remove the chillies. If you like more of a kick, carry on leaving it for 10-minute intervals and tasting it until it is perfectly spiced. Once you've removed the chillies, place in the fridge for 12 hours to infuse then enjoy.

Whiskey Orange Marmalade

This marmalade brings the scent of oranges to your cheeseboard with its bittersweet loveliness it pairs really well with cheese and who doesn't like a boozy marmalade. This is great with Pecorino.

750g (1lb 10oz) Seville oranges, washed
juice of 1 lemon
1.5kg (3lb 4oz/scant 7 cups) preserving sugar
2 rosemary sprigs, leaves very finely chopped
1 tbsp treacle (molasses)
40ml (1¼fl oz/2½ tbsp) Irish whiskey

Put the oranges and lemon juice into a large saucepan with 1.5 litres (50fl oz/6¼ cups) water and stir. Bring to the boil, then reduce the heat to a simmer. Partially cover with a lid and cook for 2½ hours, until the oranges are soft. Take the pan off the heat, remove the oranges (reserving the cooking liquid) and set aside to cool.

When the oranges are cool enough to handle, halve them and scoop the flesh and seeds back into the pan with the cooking liquid. Bring to the boil and simmer for 30 minutes.

While the cooked oranges are simmering, shred the orange peel into thin strips.

Once ready, pour the cooked orange mixture through a sieve into another large saucepan, pressing through as much pulp as possible. Stir in the peel, sugar, rosemary and treacle and slowly bring to the boil. Stir regularly, until the sugar has dissolved, then increase the heat and boil rapidly for 6–10 minutes until setting point is reached.

To check for the setting point, the marmalade should reach 105°C/221°F on a thermometer. Alternatively, place a couple of saucers in the freezer to chill. When you are ready to check the marmalade, drop a spoonful onto the cold plate and leave to cool. Once cold, drag your finger through the marmalade and if it wrinkles and leaves a trail where your finger has been, it is ready to jar. If the marmalade runs back into the gap, it needs to be boiled for longer. Repeat testing for setting point at 10-minute intervals until the marmalade is ready.

Remove the pan from the heat and add the whiskey. Mix well then set aside for about 15 minutes to cool slightly,. Stir again, then ladle into sterilised jars and seal. Store in a cool, dry place and refrigerate once opened.

Gin-pickled Cucumbers

The gorgeous fresh flavours of these pickles bring a lightness to cheese. The sharp, zesty flavours work really well on a cheese board and also add a dash of colour. Serve alongside Comté.

1 medium cucumber, cut into thin rounds
½ tsp salt
70ml (2½fl oz/scant 5 tbsp) white wine vinegar
40ml (1¼fl oz/2½ tbsp) gin
2 tbsp caster (superfine) sugar
½ tbsp mustard seeds

Place the cucumber rounds in a sieve placed over a bowl, then sprinkle over the salt. Leave to sit for 1 hour, then rinse under cold running water to remove the salt and place in a heatproof bowl. Put the vinegar, gin, sugar and mustard seeds in a saucepan with 125ml (4¼fl oz/generous ½ cup) water, and place over a medium heat until the sugar has dissolved. Pour the liquid over the cucumber and place in the fridge for at least 2 hours before serving.

Hot Honey

Hot Honey happens to be one of my favourite things to put on a cheeseboard. This sweet spiced nectar brings any cheese to life with just a drizzle.

350g (12oz) honey
2 hot fresno or scotch bonnet chillies, roughly chopped
3 small dried chillies

Put all the ingredients in a saucepan and simmer over a medium heat for 10–15 minutes to infuse the honey with the chilli flavour and heat. Remove from the heat and leave to cool, then pass the honey through a sieve to remove the peppers and seeds.

Leave the honey to sit for 30 minutes before transferring to a sterilised jar and sealing.

The Best Cheese Shops from Around the World

For a good selection of cheeses, I recommend finding your nearest cheese shop and exploring local delis too. Here are some of my favourite international cheesemongers.

The best cheese shop in the world*

Cheeses of Muswell Hill
13 Fortis Green Road,
London, N10 3HP
https://cheesesonline.co.uk

*maybe I am biased

UK

BELFAST
Arcadia Delicatessen
378 Lisburn Rd, BT9 6GL
www.arcadiadeli.co.uk

Mike's Fancy Cheeser
41 Little Donegall St, BT1 2JD
www.mfcheese.com

BRISTOL
The Bristol Cheesemonger
Unit 8 Cargo 2, Museum St,
BS1 6ZA
www.bristol-cheese.co.uk

CARDIFF
Madame Fromage
16 Nevill Street, Abergavenny,
Monmouthshire, NP7 5AD
www.madamefromage.co.uk

DUBLIN
Sheridans Cheesemonger
Multiple locations
www.sheridanscheesemongers.
com

EDINBURGH
I.J. Mellis
Multiple locations
www.mellischeese.net

GLASGOW
George Mewes Cheese
106 Byres Rd, G12 8TB
www.georgemewescheese.co.uk

LEEDS
George & Joseph Cheesemongers
140 Harrogate Rd, Chapel
Allerton, LS7 4NZ
www.georgeandjoseph.co.uk

LONDON
Kappacasein
1 Stoney St, SE1 9AA
www.kappacasein.com

La Fromagerie
Stores in Highbury, Marylebone &
Bloomsbury
www.lafromagerie.co.uk

Neal's Yard Dairy
Stores in Borough Market, Covent
Garden, Islington & Bermondsey
www.nealsyarddairy.co.uk

Paxton and Whitfield
93 Jermyn Street, SW1Y 6JE
www.paxtonandwhitfield.co.uk

The Fine Cheese Co.
Stores in Belgravia & Bath
www.finecheeseshops.co.uk

MANCHESTER
The Cheese Hamlet
706 Wilmslow Rd, Didsbury,
M20 2DW
www.thecheesehamlet.co.uk

YORKSHIRE
The Courtyard Dairy
Crows Nest Barn, Near Settle,
Austwick LA2 8AS
www.thecourtyarddairy.co.uk

Europe

AUSTRIA
Jumi
Lange G. 28, 1080 Wien, Vienna
www.jumi.lu

BELGIUM
Catherine
Rue du Midi 23, 1000, Brussels
www.fromagerie-catherine.be

Kaashuys Den Hof
Jozef Suvéestraat 6, 8000,
Bruges
www.kaashuysdenhof.be

CZECH REPUBLIC
La Formaggeria
Multiple locations
www.laformaggeria.com

FRANCE
Cremerie Normande
31 Rue Michel d'Ornano, 14640
Villers-sur-Mer, Normany

Coopérative fruitière en Val d'Arly Savoie Mont-Blanc
Les Seigneurs, 71 Chemin des Evettes, 73590 Flumet,
www.coopvaldarly.com

Fromagerie De La Fruitiere
88 Pl. de la Fruitière, 74310 Les Houches, French Alps
www.fromagerie-fruitiere.com

Alléosse
13 Rue Poncelet, 75017, Paris
www.fromage-alleosse.com

Androuët
37, rue de Verneuil, 75007, Paris
www.androuet.com

Fromagrie Barthélémy
51 Rue de Grenelle, 75007, Paris

Laurent Dubois
47 Ter Bd Saint-Germain, 75005, Paris
www.fromageslaurentdubois.fr

GREECE
Καραμανλίδικα του Φάνη ανλίδικα του Φάνη
Sokratous 1, Athina 105 52
www.karamanlidika.com

ITALY
Formaggioteca Terroir
Via dei Renai, 19, 50125 Firenze FI, Florence
www.formaggiotecaterroir.it

Peck
Via Spadari, 9, 20123, Milan
www.peck.it

Beppe and His Cheeses
Via di S. Maria del Pianto, 9A/11, 00186 Roma RM, Rome
www.beppeeisuoiformaggi.it

Cacio Della Campagna Romana
Via dei Giubbonari, 35, 00186 Roma RM, Rome

La Tradizione
Via Cipro, 8 E, 00136 Roma RM, Rome
www.latradizione.it

Paciotti Salumeria
Via Marcantonio Bragadin, 51, 00136 Roma RM, Rome
www.paciottisalumeria.it

La Bottega del Formaggio
Via Bagnoli Croci, 28, 98039 Taormina ME, Sicily
https://la-bottega-del-formaggio.business.site

Aliani Casa Del Parmigiano
Campo Cesare Battisti/Bella Viena, San Polo 214, 30125 Venezia VE, Venice
www.casadelparmigiano.ve.it

I Tre Mercanti
Calle al Ponte de la Guerra, 5364, 30122 Venezia VE, Venice
www.itremercanti.it

NETHERLANDS
T Kaaswinkeltje
Lange Tiendeweg 30, 2801 KH , Gouda

NORWAY
Fromagerie
Valkyriegata 9, 0366, Oslo
www.fromagerie.no

SPAIN
Poncelet Cheese Bar
Calle de José Abascal, 61, 28003, Madrid
www.ponceletcheesebar.es

Quesería Cultivo
Conde Duque, 15, 28015, Madrid
www.queseriacultivo.com

SWIZERLAND
Fromagerie Dupasquier
Rue de Cornavin 1, 1201
www.fromageriedupasquier.ch

Tritt Käse
Limmatstrasse 231, 8005, Zürich
www.tritt.ch

Welschland Ladeli
Zweierstrasse 56, 8004, Zürich
www.welschland.com

North America

ATLANTA
Star Provisions
1460 Ellsworth Industrial Blvd NW, Atlanta, GA 30318
www.starprovisions.com

CALIFORNIA
The Cheese Store of Beverley Hills
419 N Beverly Dr, Beverly Hills, CA 90210
www.cheesestorebh.com

DTLA Cheese
317 S Broadway #45, Los Angeles, CA 90013
www.dtlacheese.com

The Cheese Board Collective
1512 Shattuck Ave, Berkeley, CA 94709
www.cheeseboardcollective.coop

Cheese Plus
2001 Polk St, San Francisco, CA 94109
www.cheeseplus.com

La Fromagerie
101 Montgomery St, San Francisco, CA 94104
lafromageriesf.com

COLORADO
Cured
1825 Pearl St Ste B, Boulder, CO 80302
www.curedboulder.com

ILLINOIS
Beautiful Rind
> 2211 N Milwaukee Ave, Chicago, IL 60647 www.beautifulrind.com

MAINE
The Cheese Shop of Portland
> 107 Washington Ave #1, Portland, ME 04101 www.thecheeseshopofportland.com

MASSACHUSETTS
Rubiner's Cheesemongers & Grocers
> 264 Main St, Great Barrington, MA 01230 www.rubiners.com

NEW YORK
Bedford Cheese Shop
> 67 Irving Pl, NY 10003 www.bedfordcheeseshop.com

Saxelby Cheesemongers
> 75 9th Ave, NY 10011 www.saxelbycheese.com

TEXAS
Antonelli's Cheese Shop
> 500 Park Blvd, Austin, TX 78751 www.antonellischeese.com

WASHINGTON
Big John's PFI
> 1608 S Dearborn St, Seattle, WA 98144 www.bigjohnspfi.com

DeLaurenti Food & Wine
> 1435 1st Avenue, Seattle, WA, 98101, https://delaurenti.com

Murray's Cheese
> Multiple locations www.murrayscheese.com

CANADA
Country Cheese Company
> 289 Kingston Rd E #3, Ajax, ON L1Z 0K5 https://countrycheesecompany.com

C'est Cheese Please
> 40 Grand Ave N, Cambridge, ON N1S 2K8 www.cestcheeseplease.ca

Daniel's Cheese and Deli
> 250 Thompson Dr, Cambridge, ON N1T 2E3 www.danielscheese.com

Central & South America

BRAZIL
A Queijaria
> R. Aspicuelta, 35 - Vila Madalena, São Paulo - SP, 05433-010 www.aqueijariavirtual.com.br

DELIKA
R. Pedro Cristi
> 89 - Pinheiros, São Paulo - SP, 05421-040

CHILE
Quesos Don Rafa
> Mercado Tirso De Molina Local 158, RM Santiago

El Rey Del Queso de Cabra
> José Santos Ossa 2488, Antofagasta

MEXICO
La Esperanza
> Av Moliere 352, Polanco, Polanco II Secc, Miguel Hidalgo, 11550 Mexico City

Le Fromager
> Calle Alejandro Dumas Dumas 125, Mexico City

Unilac Bodega de Quesos
> Fernando Montes de Oca 120, Colonia Condesa, Cuauhtémoc, 06140 México City

South Africa

Giovanni's Deli World
> 103 Main Rd, Green Point, Cape Town, 8051 https://giovannisdeli.co.za

Bryanston Organic Market
> 40 Culross Rd, Bryanston, Sandton, 2191, Johannesburg www.bryanstonmarket.co.za

Cheese Gourmet
> 3rd Avenue, 71A 7th St, Linden, Johannesburg, 2195

Cremalat
> Martin Cres Street Greenhills Industrial Estate Tunney Ext 6 Elandsfontein, Bedfordview, 1429 www.cremalat.co.za

Cremona Cheese
> 21 Prospect Rd, Tshepisong, Roodepoort, 1734 www.cremonacheese.co.za

La Marina Foods
> 7 Platinum Dr, Longmeadow, North Business Park, Lethabong, 2090 www.lamarinafoods.co.za

The Cheese Shop
> Hoekplaats 384-Jr, Centurion, 0083

Asia

CHINA

La Formaggeria
1250 Huaihai Zhong Road
Xujiahui District
https://www.brazzaleshanghai.
com

IL Bel Paese
www.ilbelpaese.com.hk

La Cremerie
4 Swatow St, Wan Chai,
Hong Kong

SINGAPORE

Cheese Ark
49 Stirling Rd, #01-489,
Singapore 141049
www.thecheeseark.com

La Fromagerie
5 Mohamed Sultan Rd,
Singapore 239014
www.gourmetshop.com.sg

So France
7 Fraser Street Duo Galleria
#01-51/56 Bugis MRT, 189356
www.so-france.sg

The Cheese Artisans
www.cheeseartisans.com.sg

THAILAND

Cheesequintessence
21 On Nut 82 Alley, Prawet,
10250, Bangkok
www.cheesequintessence.com

El Mercado
490 Phai Singto Alley, Khlong
Toei, Bangkok 10110
www.elmercadobangkok.com

Gourmé Italia
Soi Ruamrudee Community,
Lumphini, Pathum Wan District,
Bangkok 10330

Australia

MELBOURNE

Maker & Monger
Prahran Market, Stall 98/163
Commercial Rd,
South Yarra VIC 3141
www.makerandmonger.com.au

Milk the Cow
323 Lygon St, Carlton VIC 3053
www.milkthecow.com.au

SYDNEY

Deli Fresco
Shop 1008, Pacific Highway,
Hornsby NSW 2077
http://www.delifresco.com.au

Gourmet Life
52-60 New South Head Rd,
Edgecliff, NSW 2027
www.gourmetlife.com.au

Penny's Cheese Shop
Shop 6/127-139 Macleay St, Potts
Point, NSW 2011
www.pennyscheeseshop.com.au

The Artisan Cheese Room
1/40 E Esplanade, Manly NSW 2095
www.theartisancheeseroom.com.
au

PERTH

Boatshed Market
40 Jarrad St, Cottesloe WA 6011
www.boatshedmarket.com.au

QUEENSLAND

Kenilworth Dairies
41 Charles St, Kenilworth
QLD 4570
www.kenilworthdairies.com.au

TASMANIA

Bruny Island Cheese Co
1807 Bruny Island Main Rd,
Great Bay TAS 7150
https://www.brunyislandcheese.
com.au

Other stockists

Abel & Cole
https://www.abelandcole.co.uk

Belazu
https://www.belazu.com

Brindisa
www.brindisa.com

Celtic Bakery
https://thecelticbakers.co.uk

Crosta & Mollica
https://www.crostamollica.com

Daylesford Organic
https://www.daylesford.com

Exotic Fruits
https://exoticfruits.co.uk

Fine Food Specialist
https://www.finefoodspecialist.co.uk

Gail's
https://gailsbread.co.uk

Miller's
https://www.artisanbiscuits.co.uk

Peter's Yard
https://www.petersyard.com/shop

Riverford
https://www.riverford.co.uk

Ross & Ross
https://rossandrossgifts.co.uk

Seggiano
https://seggiano.com

Taste of Sicily
https://www.tasteofsicily.co.uk

Tracklements
https://www.tracklements.co.uk